Leaders Rave About...

Grow Through It & Lead

"Spark Plug certainly has an appropriate name because he knows how to stimulate action in one's life. Not only does he THINK BIG, but I think through this book he will inspire many others to do the same. It is rare for a young man to have so much wisdom and to be able to impart it to others."

—Benjamin S. Carson, Sr., M.D., Bestselling Author of *Think Big* and *Gifted Hands*
Director of Pediatric Neurosurgery
Professor of Neurological Surgery, John Hopkins

"The contagious enthusiasm of The Spark Plug shines brightly in this inspiring new book that speaks to overcoming adversity and reaching one's full potential."

—Vince Dooley
Former Head Football Coach and Athletic Director, University of Georgia

"A breath of fresh air! That's exactly what I felt when I read this book. Everyone needs to be reminded that they can prevail in any situation because they already have what it takes."

—Tiffany Cochran
Reporter/News Anchor for WXIA-TV

"Since life is so full of hurdles, I'd like to commend 'The Spark Plug' for writing a book of inspiration that can help you leap over them!"

—Jimmy Carnes
Head U.S. Olympic Track and Field Coach 1980
Ex. Dir. U.S. Track Coaches Association

"A sound and solid book that is both easy and enjoyable to read. It is filled with memorable anecdotes that help you reflect on the things that are really important in life. It also reminds people that no matter how tough things may seem, there's always a way out."

—Billy "White Shoes" Johnson
Director of Programs, Atlanta Falcons, All-Time NFL Team

Leaders' comments continued on following page...

"Thank you 'Spark Plug' for writing a heartfelt and priceless book that speaks to the reader's potential! I'm sure it will help make a difference in the lives of the people who are privileged to read it."

—Fred Gibson
Asst. Dean of Instruction, DeKalb Technical College

"This book is entertaining, but most of all, inspirational! And if you haven't heard 'The Spark Plug' speak, you are missing out on an unforgettable and motivational happening!"

—Carol Hacker
Author of *The High Cost of Low Morale—and What to Do About It*

GROW
THROUGH IT &
LEAD

Tap into and Develop
Your Potential and Open the
Gateway to Your Future

THE SPARK PLUG
with Jacqueline Benjamin Thomas

A *Possibility Press* Book

GROW
THROUGH IT &
LEAD

THE SPARK PLUG
with Jacqueline Benjamin Thomas

Copyright © 2007 by Anthony Thomas
ISBN 0-938716-67-0

1   2   3   4   5   6   7   8   9   10

Published by
Possibility Press
info@possibilitypress.com

Manufactured in the United States of America

Dedication

Ralph Waldo Emerson said, "The glory of friendship is not the outstretched hand, nor the kindly smile, nor the joy of companionship; it is the spiritual inspiration that comes to one when he discovers that someone else believes in him and is willing to trust him."

To Bryce, a fourth grader, who is so full of potential; he's an inspiration to me.

My community has an outreach program that encourages its citizens to become in-school mentors. Since becoming Bryce's mentor, I have painfully discovered that he has already experienced situations that seem too overwhelming even for adults to bear. Hopefully, one day, he will read this book and be reminded that not only can he dream impossible dreams, but he can also achieve them.

Acknowledgment

It would be ludicrous for us to suggest that we have written this book solely from the depths of our own souls. Therefore, we would like to thank many of the people who have crossed our path. Without your influence, these pages would have remained unwritten.

Whether it was through a book, over the phone, or face-to-face, you have given us experiences that have inspired us in some way or another. The space in this book is not large enough to hold the names of each and every one of you. Nevertheless, please know that your contribution is appreciated, and we sincerely thank you again from the bottom of our hearts!

Webster's Dictionary Says...

(spärk · plug´) 2. Informal. a person who leads, inspires, or animates a group.

*   *   *

At this very moment, some people are giving up hope, losing confidence. They don't believe they can make it just one more day.

In order to be the best we can be and do the best we can do, we all need a little encouragement on a *daily* basis. We need someone to cheer us on when we face the most difficult times. Our deepest desire is that you receive some inspiration from this book to help you make it over the next hurdle on this adventure called *"life."* As Johann G. Von Herder reminded us, "Without inspiration, the best powers of the mind remain dormant; there is a fuel in us that needs to be ignited by sparks."

*   *   *

"**D**eep in the recesses of every human soul, a mighty power is always at work. It serves as a constant reminder to press onward, achieve more, be more, give more. Until we take the first step toward rearranging our lifestyle in a more positive way, this mighty power will cause us to become as restless as a pregnant woman, held hostage by the piercing pain of intense labor. Giving birth to positive change will not come without shedding old habits, some old friends, old fears, and old ways of thinking. It will not come without tossing and turning, sometimes even crying a river of tears, or perhaps lying awake in the still of the night, staring at the ceiling, praying for answers. Answers will come and positive changes will too. Though often wrapped in struggles and disappointments, torment and rejection, heartaches and pain, sickness and suffering, weeping and wailing...still, they come."

—Jacqueline Benjamin Thomas

Contents

Instilling Hope in Others

"Compared to what we ought to be, we are only half awake. Our fires are dampened, our drafts are checked, we are making use of only a small part of our mental and physical resources."
—William James—

After I published my first book, *125 Ways to Add a Spark to Your Day*, I started getting calls from corporations and organizations whose leaders all seemed to be faced with the same dilemma. "Can you come in and *inspire* the troops?" they so often requested. Some of them asked, "While you're at it, can you say something about leadership?"

These requests heightened my interest in leadership, leading me to Mercer University where I obtained a degree in Organization Leadership. I learned that most companies and organizations struggled with the same issues: practicing effective leadership and getting team members excited about what they're doing.

An effective leader knows there is nothing more powerful than instilling hope in others. They know that inspiration helps people tap into the 90 percent of their ability that lies dormant within. As William James wrote: "Compared to what we ought to be, we are only half awake. Our fires are dampened, our drafts are checked, we are making use of only a small part of our mental and physical resources." Tapping into unused physical, mental, and spiritual resources helps people become more confident. It increases their self-esteem and gives them the strength and courage to persevere during tough times.

More than ever before, organizations need people to lead, coach, and inspire others to tap into their potential—and stay in the race for the long haul. Organizations also need leaders who understand that leadership is *all about the people*. Without good people doing good things, organizations perish.

The purpose of this book is to ignite a spark within you. Hopefully, you'll be *inspired* to become all that you were meant to be—in your work and personal life—when times are good and when times are tough.

To your bright future,

The Spark Plug

Being There for Others

As I travel, speaking to various groups and organizations, the number one question I am constantly asked is: "Can you say something to our people to help them deal with the tough times we are facing as a nation, as well as an organization?"

No matter where we are in our lives right now, we all need motivation and inspiration. They are as essential as the air we breathe; therefore, always strive to *encourage* others.

In my travels around the world, meeting thousands of people, I have found that everyone wants praise, encouragement, and to be part of something worthwhile. Therefore, my primary goal in writing this book is to give you hope and encouragement.

When it comes to encouragement, we need all we can get. All great leaders encourage and inspire their troops to victory. Encouragement is the mother of all achievement. If the encouraging words in this book spark you to do great things, then I've done what I've set out to do.

As long as I can remember, even as a little boy growing up in Columbia, South Carolina, I knew I had to do something to make a difference. I didn't know what it was going to be. I just knew I had to do *something*. I literally began to look for ways in which I could make a difference. As poet Joann Oswald wrote, "I started to think about the person in me and what I could do and what I could be." I discovered that I had a desire to lead and take charge of things, even when I didn't want the responsibility.

When I was about fourteen, I had an experience that changed my life forever. It involved a sad story of a little six-year-old boy named Jay. He was a cute little kid with curly red hair, freckles, and an easy smile. He was also very outgoing and well-mannered. What was amazing about Jay, though, was that he already knew how to cook full-course meals! Unfortunately, Jay was often a victim of child abuse at the hands of his own mother.

One day, I saw him as he was on his way to the local convenience store, walking at a quick pace in my direction. I was on my way to the neighborhood tennis courts to practice my game. Calling out to him, as I always did, I shouted, "How's it going, Jay?"

He yelled back, "Fine, but I can't talk right now. I have to go to the store for my mom."

After we got to within a few feet of each other, I noticed that something in his hair made it look all matted together.

I inquired, "Jay, what's that in your hair?"

He retorted, "Nothing, I can't talk right now or I'll get into trouble. I have to go to the store for my mom."

He started to cry.

I asked, "Jay, what's wrong?"

Once again, his reply was the same.

"Nothing!"

As I got even closer to him, I saw blood running down his ear from a gash he had in the top of his head. I was frightened for him because he was losing blood. I told him to come with me *immediately* to the management office of the apartment complex where we lived, so he could, at least, get some bandages.

Jay emphatically said, "No, I can't. I'll get into trouble."

After pleading with him, to no avail, to come with me, I decided to run to the management office as fast as I could, so they could call an ambulance or the police. I knew I *had* to do something. When I arrived at the office, I told the manager what I had witnessed. She quickly called an ambulance. We got into her car and she speedily drove up the hill to the nearby convenience store.

When we walked into the store, we saw little Jay at the counter purchasing a pack of cigarettes for his mother. It was one of the most disturbing sights I had ever seen in my life. This little innocent human being standing there with matted hair, a gash in the top of his head with blood running down his ear, still determined to obey his abusive mother at any cost.

I'll never forget what little Jay told us that day.

He bravely said, "You know, when my mom hit me on top of my head with that belt buckle, I didn't even cry."

At that point, all the adults who were looking on broke down in tears.

A few weeks later, on the evening before it was time to go to court to testify on little Jay's behalf, I remember walking around the apartment complex. I was asking the kids who knew he had been beaten by his mother if *they* were going to court.

They all replied, "No, we can't go. Our parents won't let us." I remember being extremely disappointed with both my friends *and* their parents. Albert Einstein was right when he said, "The world is not dangerous because of those who do harm, but because of those who look at it without doing anything."

None of the other kids in the neighborhood made it to court to save little Jay from his abusive mother. I was the only person who testified on his behalf. Amazingly, his mother was still granted custody of him after this horrible episode. A few days later, they moved away and I never saw or heard from little Jay again. I often think about him and talk about him every now and then in my presentations. My prayer is that somehow things have turned around for him. He's one of the reasons I endeavor to inspire others as much as I can. That early experience made a huge impact on my life.

Just as I was there for little Jay, I want to be here for you, too, via this book. I hope it inspires you to do more for others.

—1—

Change Your Attitude, Young Man!

"Life will never *be fair all by itself. We need to look for the good,
take charge of the challenges, and grow through them."*
—The Spark Plug—

The year was 1977. I turned thirteen and began to realize I had developed somewhat of an attitude problem. No one could tell me anything! I had all the answers, or so I thought. But one day, the intensity of my mother's often-repeated words suddenly began to make sense. Almost weekly, she told me, "Change your attitude, young man!" It got to the point where I could no longer ignore these five simple, yet powerful words. It was time for a positive change.

One sunny spring day, I decided to let an afternoon of tennis rescue me from the weekend routine at home. My thinking was always clearer when I was battling it out on the courts—I was focused. I thought that if I worked at it hard enough, finding a solution to my attitude problem would be a cinch. While quickly gathering my tennis gear, I caught a glimpse of my mother in the kitchen giving me the eye as she washed dishes. She was giving me the serious look— the look that always speaks louder than words. I knew it was my cue to disappear. Hurriedly, I made a mad dash for the front door.

"See you later, Mom," I quickly shouted. "I'll make sure I'm back before dinner." Out the door I went, heading out into the gentle warmth of the sun.

On my way to the courts, I stopped by the tennis shop at the mall and picked up my three freshly strung Wilson Jack Kramer tennis rackets. A feeling of exhilaration was rapidly growing inside of me. I couldn't wait to get to the courts. It was a great day for tennis!

I tried to dismiss my mother's words, but they continued to painfully echo in my mind. "You need to change your attitude, young man!" The ache in my heart was unbearable. I began to wonder…now, what will it actually take to change my attitude? What's the big deal, anyway? Why is my mother always on my back about it? Why is this *attitude* business making my mother fume? More specifically, how can I take control of something that seems so uncontrollable? I had no idea I could control my attitude the same way I controlled my backhand.

Excuse Me, *Your Attitude Is Showing!*

We all live complex lives. Not long ago, I was on the phone with Hilda Smith, a good friend of mine. We were sharing information about interesting books we had read. She talked about the book, *The Road Less Traveled.* Scott Peck, the author, wrote, "Life is difficult…." I told her that those three words were some of the truest words ever written. One of the lessons children need to learn early on is that life isn't fair, but that's okay. The sooner they learn to accept this, the better off they'll be. Unfortunately, too many adults are still expecting life to be fair. But life will *never* be fair all by itself. We need to look for the good, take charge of the challenges, and grow through them.

We're all going to face circumstances that test everything we believe to be true. Sometimes, we're going to experience situations that come without warning and may seem totally unfair. But no matter how bleak things may appear, we need to deal with them head on, being as fair as we can through the process. This is the only way we can accomplish what we originally set out to do. Resist any temptation to use the challenge as an excuse and you will prevail.

To triumph over tough times doesn't mean we must wear a pasted-on smile, operate in a panic mode, or walk around in denial—oblivious to what's really happening in our lives. During these times, it would be unrealistic to expect anyone to be jovial at every tick tock of the clock. No one needs to feel obligated to dance through every disappointment or stand up and cheer about the stress and strain of every heavy burden. There are times when our unexpected temporary setbacks will totally knock us off our feet, rip our hearts out, and turn our whole world upside down. Believe me, I've never felt like leading a cheering section at these times in my life, and you probably haven't either.

To triumph means having *faith* and *confidence* that our life is unfolding as it needs to. It means standing our ground and fighting for our dreams, despite rejections and fears. It means standing up for those who can't stand up for themselves. It's about being determined to find a pearl of goodness in every situation, even when it seems as if there is none to be found. When times are tough, our attitude will largely determine whether we win or lose.

Whether it's good, bad, or indifferent, wherever you are right now, your attitude is showing. When you treat someone differently based on appearance, race, physical ability, financial worth, or educational level, your attitude is showing. When you pick a certain style of clothing over another, your attitude is showing. Whether you choose to surround yourself with a cloud of dismay or wrap yourself in a blanket of hope, your attitude is always showing.

The Power to Choose

Our attitude and the decisions we make often share a common thread. More often than not, it's our attitude that governs the choices we make and how they affect our future. Where we are at this particular moment in life has been primarily determined by the choices we've made along the way. Whether we're aware of it or not, our actions and decisions really do shape our destiny. My wife came across a Japanese proverb that stresses this point even further. It warns us that "The reputation of a thousand years may be determined by the conduct of one hour." How true.

The power to choose is awesome. When we fail to make decisions that will richly fertilize our lives, we've automatically made a choice to stay where we are. Until we accept the fact that we are, at times, our own stumbling block, we may never move forward, see beyond our circumstances, or prosper. Many times, the walls of disappointment, defeat, and regret that overshadow us are crafted by the choices we have made.

Some of you may be saying, "I'm stuck in a rut and disgusted with my life and this economy. I'll never find a job that will give me the life I want." Or you may be saying to yourself, "Because of this sluggish economy, now is not a good time to start a new business...." In his thought-provoking book, *The Achievement Factors,* Gene Griessman reveals to us that we grow into our own expectations. If you're not expecting much of yourself, you probably won't receive or accomplish very much. The reason is as simple as this: The less you expect of yourself, the less you will *do* to meet your *already* lowered expectations.

Successful people know there's not a lack of money in the world; there's only a lack of ambition. So don't give up, sit down, or manufacture a sour outlook on life. It won't get you anywhere. "Keep your face to the sunshine and you cannot see the shadows," wrote Helen Keller. Take action—get into motion—and watch how things begin to fall into place.

I once met a homeless man who told me that his wife had been unfaithful to him. According to him, she had literally emptied his pockets and ruined his life.

"It's all her fault," he complained. "On top of that, she divorced me and took everything," he added.

"How long have you been divorced?" I asked.

"Twenty years," he snarled, with a faraway look in his eyes.

This poor man was still holding his wife responsible for his "homeless" condition. Steeped in his own self-pity, he had frittered away twenty years of his life and was in grave danger of wasting many more.

If you think your dreadful past is holding you back, you are denying the present and disrespecting your future. If you claim someone, a certain situation, or an experience is holding you back, then you don't understand how creative, intelligent, talented, and gifted you really are. You're not taking responsibility for who you really are. Without a doubt, there's a purpose for your life, and the only person who can keep it from you is reading this book. If you're afraid of looking foolish, stumbling, or falling in your quest for a better quality of life, just remember that uncomfortable, character-building experiences are necessary for growth.

Speaking of a better quality of life…a few years ago, I discovered that my mother went back to finish high school when she was twenty-one. A series of heartbreaking events had interrupted her education. While suffering spousal abuse and having the responsibility of raising three small children on her own, she set out to construct a better future for us as well as herself. She was called stupid and dumb for being in the tenth grade at twenty-one, when the average age for a tenth grader is fifteen or sixteen. Determined to succeed, she refused to give in to the constant public humiliation from her fellow classmates. She didn't allow it to break her stride.

Eventually, my mother graduated from high school. Many years later, she graduated from college and has since earned two masters degrees! Diligently, she planted seeds of sacrifice and overcame the obstacles that she had once allowed to hold her hostage. She expanded her boundaries, strengthened her confidence, and chose to believe that she could accomplish *much* more for her family and herself.

To Degree, or Not to Degree—*That Is the Question*

Some of you may contend that your lack of education or degree is holding you back. "If only I had finished college, or even gone to college, I would have a better chance of reaching my goals," some may grumble. This statement may or may not be true for you. It all depends on what your goals are. The names on the list of successful business professionals, entrepreneurs, and entertainers who didn't attend or finish college are too numerous to mention.

I know that becoming knowledgeable in an area where we intend to excel is as essential to us as oxygen. Expanding our knowledge can open the door to unlimited possibilities. However, the best education does not always come with a formal degree attached to it. Just study the lives of people like Vivien Thomas, the celebrated Johns Hopkins University surgical teacher. With only a high school diploma, he trained many of the world's leading surgeons in the 1950s and '60s. Later on, he received an Honorary Doctorate from Johns Hopkins for his groundbreaking work with the renowned heart surgeon, Dr. Alfred Blalock, with whom he *developed* the field of cardiac surgery.

Then consider the late Dave Thomas, founder of the Wendy's restaurant chain. He didn't receive his high school diploma until he had already achieved international success in the restaurant business.

There's a gold mine of inexpensive books, CDs, and DVDs filled with valuable and helpful information right at our fingertips. Our experiences are also exceptional teachers, and training is available on almost any topic imaginable. Having a degree doesn't always mean we're educated. It's basically a license to work in the real world.

The point is many people have fabricated a horde of excuses for not moving forward. They use excuses in a futile attempt to help pardon themselves from feeling guilty about their lack of progress. They find comfort in blaming others for the life they've created. The trouble is blame only weakens their power to make positive changes. It gives them an excuse for not taking responsibility for their own actions. Yet, blame can never erase the years that have been carelessly traded for a life of advanceless inertia.

No Time to Whine

For some of us, being sincerely grateful for the things we already have is as rare as seeing a shooting star. It's so easy to forget or overlook the little things that mean so much. My wife and I have an 85-year-old friend named Miriam Manning, who resides in a nursing home in Griffin, Georgia. We have known her for eight years. When we first met her, she had already lost one leg because of diabetes. Now, she has lost both of her legs to that disease. But in spite of that horrific loss, she has not turned bitter. Not once have we heard her whine or complain about her situation. Each time we have visited her, she has always had a good attitude and a positive outlook on life. Miriam has to patiently *wait* for someone to bathe her. She has to *wait* for someone to physically pick her up and put her in a wheelchair when she wants to leave her room. She has to *wait* for someone to bring her meals. She has to *wait* for someone to dress her. She has to *wait* for someone to visit her. She can never leave her bed on her own!

It was E.E. Cummings who said, "The most wasted of all days is one without laughter." Miriam is a shining example of someone who makes the best of what most of us would consider a very dismal situation. She has retained the spirit of love and laughter.

The World Bank has reported that of the six billion people on the planet, two billion get by on less than two dollars a day, while one billion gets by on less than one dollar a day. Can you even imagine getting by on such a small amount of money? Some of you may be saying, "It's different in other parts of the world, you don't need that much to survive." Well, after traveling around the world, I know first-hand that it is difficult to survive on less than one or two dollars a day no matter where you live. I think it comes down to what Mahatma Gandhi cautioned us about many decades ago: "We have enough for every man's need, but not enough for every man's greed."

We take too much for granted. Some of us constantly sob, whimper, and whine about not being able to satisfy our ego. Many of us are involved in a tremendous opportunity, but, nonetheless, we still make excuses and continue to place blame. As Jay Rifenbary, bestselling author of *No Excuse!* says, "When the going gets tough, the weak blame."

Stop right now and get a pen and a sheet of paper.

Take a few moments to identify the obstacles in your life that are keeping you from moving forward. Think about it, but don't take too long. Jot down what and who they are then write in full detail how they are hindering you from making progress. Be honest, there's no reason for you to hold back or be ashamed. We're talking about your future. This brief, yet important exercise is for your eyes only. Look closely at what you've written. Analyze every single excuse.

Does that sheet of paper have any power to keep you from your purpose? Do you hear voices yelling from it demanding that you stay where you are and not move forward? Does it have powerful hands tightly locked together like a steel chain, forming a barricade to hold you back?

I don't think so!

If you still think other people or circumstances can keep you from your purpose, you're deluding yourself. If you believe you cannot rise up from where you are and move on, you're misleading yourself. You're already gifted with each and every attribute necessary to reach your goals. It's your responsibility to develop them by getting wrapped up in the art of doing. In other words, take action.

What's Your Problem?

In 1992, I decided I wanted to be a professional speaker. I yearned to inspire people to dream big dreams and reach for the impossible. Unfortunately, I had a small problem. Some people may call it a monumental one. "What was the problem?" you ask? I was afraid to stand up and give a speech in public. Deep down in my heart, I knew nothing could stop me from doing what I believed I was put on this planet to do. Nevertheless, my fear of failing was keeping me from taking the first step.

So, to overcome my fear of public speaking, I started reading books about it. To test the waters, I started speaking to little kids first; they are less judgmental. They just want to know you care. Eventually, I joined a speaking organization that helped me build a firm foundation in the fundamentals of public speaking. After that, I joined my state speakers association, as well as the National Speakers Association, which is part of an international organization of professional speakers.

You May Not Be the First Choice

I now travel around the country and abroad, speaking for many leading Fortune 500 companies and governmental agencies on leadership, diversity, and motivation.

The highlight of my speaking career came when I received a phone call from a gentleman who represented a group that wanted me to speak.

He said, "Spark Plug, we really enjoyed you at our State Conference, and if you are available, we would really love to have you in Greensboro, North Carolina at our Southeastern Conference."

He continued, "I want you to know, however, that you weren't our first choice as the keynote speaker." I was a little taken aback by his brutal honesty.

Nevertheless, I summoned up the courage to timidly ask him, "By the way, who was your first choice?"

He replied quite enthusiastically, "Oh, President Jimmy Carter." At this point, I simultaneously felt stunned and elated.

I've always been quick witted so I interjected, "Let me get this straight, if you can't get a former President, (now Nobel Peace Prize Winner) call 'The Spark Plug.'"

He responded, "That's pretty much it."

The Door Is Already Open— *Walk Through It*

In the free world, no one has to live a stagnant, unproductive life that lacks growth and creativity. Just seize the opportunity at hand and make it happen. History has recorded the lives of countless heroes who have been positive examples of succeeding against all odds, making a way out of no way. Many have made extreme sacrifices so that we have the freedom and opportunity to pursue our goals. And much blood has been shed so that we can live an abundant life. Edward Judson wrote, "If you succeed without suffering, it is because someone suffered for you; if you suffer without succeeding, it is in order that someone else may succeed after you."

Success has been engraved in your past, present, and future. You are an important piece to life's puzzle. Your contribution is vital. Your children, grandchildren, cousins, brothers, sisters, nephews, and nieces are counting on you to complete your mission because they need to stand on your shoulders. The entire world is cheering you on in this race with monumental banners that read, "You can make it. Don't give up! Keep going!" It may not be as easy as 1–2–3 for us to find out where we fit in this great big world, but it is certainly our responsibility to stay alert for clues. In the meantime, do your best and give it your all every day in whatever you're doing. No work is ever in vain!

There is a grand design and a purpose for your life that will greatly impact the lives of others in ways you could never imagine. It just doesn't matter what is thrown in your path; you can overcome it. You were born to overcome every single obstacle that comes your way. As the ambitious ant completes its mission of gathering food for the icy cold winter, you, too, can complete your mission. The tiny ant takes one faithful step at a time, one morsel of delicate food at a time, and slowly builds a warehouse of nourishment.

Yes, timing is crucial. I have painfully discovered and accepted the fact that the world has its own built-in timetable. There is nothing we can do to *force* it to operate. Scientists can't make summer come immediately after a cold winter. We must first experience the rebirth of nature in spring. Before grapes can become vintage wine, they must first be squeezed and crushed. After preparation is completed, the critical *timing* element is set in motion.

There are times when you just have to wait, but you need to *work* while you wait. Philip Simmons is a master wrought iron craftsman who is known for his contribution to the beautification of Charleston, South Carolina. His commissioned public sculptures are featured at the National Museum and the Smithsonian Institution. My wife and I had the pleasure of meeting this great American treasure at his home while we were in Charleston on one of our weekend getaways. The following quote became Mr. Simmons' motto: "If you want your prayers answered, get off your knees and hustle."

Prepare yourself to take full advantage of your opportunity. Every incident that occurs in your life is preparation for the next event. A wise person wrote, "It is better to be prepared and not have an opportunity than to have an opportunity and not be prepared." Every single circumstance that is allowed to come your way has *opportunity* written all over it. Your breakthrough may be wrapped in something you absolutely abhor. Sammy Davis, Jr. initially hated the song, "Candy Man." When he first heard it, he refused to sing it because he believed it sounded too much like a kiddie song. After its release, it became his biggest hit as well as his signature song.

Unfortunately, I didn't find any answers on that sunny spring day when I decided to flee to the tennis courts. Nevertheless, it was the beginning of a journey of seeking, growing, stumbling, and falling that brought me to where I am today. The bottom line is this: When times are tough, the key to our success or failure depends on our attitude.

"If faith that was to have moved mountains is having difficulty moving molehills, it is not because it is powerless. It's because puny, partial, tentative action hasn't given faith a chance to reveal its dynamic properties."

—Roy O. McClain

—2—

Catch the Vision and Soar!

"Eagles like you aren't meant to stay in the nest;
they're created to soar."
—The Spark Plug—

Everything begins with a dream or an idea. Occasionally, someone gets an idea and develops an invention or a business concept that dramatically improves people's lives. A flick of a switch to turn on the lights, the computer, DVD, cell phone, and the turn of a key to start the car—all of these modern conveniences started with a dream or an idea.

Just as it does for anything worthwhile, it requires a great deal of fortitude to hold on to your dream and make it a reality. I have a great deal of admiration for people who held on to their dream and never let go, regardless of countless setbacks and disappointments. Numerous biographies have been written about the courage of dreamers who changed the world, setting it on a new course.

I often think about astronaut, Ronald E. McNair, who was interested in science fiction as a young child. He became one of NASA's shining stars. Sadly, the Space Shuttle Challenger explosion in 1986 ended his life, along with the lives of six other courageous colleagues. Nevertheless, they all left legacies of courage, inspiration, and excellence.

I'm reminded of a story that Ron's brother, Carl, shared with me about growing up in Lake City, South Carolina. He and Ron were huge *Star Trek* fans. They watched the program with great curiosity and amazement, just as millions of other kids did at that time. Carl stated that Ron didn't just *watch Star Trek*; he took it a step further. At the end of every episode, Ron would exclaim with unbridled enthusiasm, "One of these days, I'm going to be in space!"

Carl often quipped, "Yeah—right. Sure you are."

Ron would then reply, "I will; just wait and see!"

Well, to make a long story short, Ron became one of NASA's first African-American astronauts, and he was a pioneer who helped to broaden the world's frontiers. Carl is a successful businessman and founder of the Ronald E. McNair Foundation in Atlanta, Georgia. He keeps his brother's dream alive, traveling around the country, encouraging young people to pursue careers in math, science, and space exploration.

In Studs Turkel's book, *Coming of Age,* he told a story about a woman who always wanted to get her college degree. At sixty-eight, most people are already retired and settled down. The young lady Mr. Turkel wrote about had loftier ambitions. She decided it didn't matter what it would take—she was finally going to start college and get that long-awaited, overdue college degree. As I read her story, I was deeply inspired by her sheer determination to accomplish her goal, toward which she toiled for eighteen long years. She happily received her degree from Harvard at the glorious and astonishing age of eighty-six years young!

During Sam Walton's early years as the founder of Wal-Mart, the people at K-mart, the dominant department store at that time, laughed at Sam and said he wouldn't last six months. Today, Wal-Mart is closing their regular stores to open Super Centers, while K-Mart has merged with Sears, trying to recover from filing bankruptcy in 2002. I don't think anyone is laughing now.

I love these stories. Remember Mr. Rogers? The *Mr. Rogers' Neighborhood* show wasn't picked up by one of the major networks because they told him that anyone hosting a children's show *must* wear a costume. Nevertheless, *Mr. Rogers' Neighborhood* was one of the longest running children's programs in television history. In 2001, Fred Rogers retired after serving as the show's host for 33 years. When he passed away in 2003, it was a sad day in the "neighborhood." However, he left a legacy of kindness and inspiration to millions of children and parents around the world.

I sincerely believe that if you hold on to your dream long enough, you can make it become a reality. Dismiss what the doubters say. Work hard and smart, find a mentor, and balance your personal and professional lives. You cannot and will not be denied true success because it lies in the journey.

My dream was to travel the globe and inspire others with a message of hope. I wanted to remind people that they have everything within themselves needed to conquer every mountain. Through hard work, persistence, pain, and commitment, and loving what you do, it can happen for you too.

Faith—*Taking a Giant Leap*

How often do we really exercise faith or take a leap into the unknown? Author Roy O. McClain wrote, "If faith that was to have moved mountains is having difficulty moving molehills, it is not because it is powerless. It's because puny, partial, tentative action hasn't given faith a chance to reveal its dynamic properties." Faith means believing in something even though we have no evidence! It kicks in and acts as a power booster during tough times. When you feel as if you have taken all you can handle, faith says wait patiently while being confident that whatever you're seeking will be brought to fruition. You don't know when or how it will occur; you just know it's bound to happen—it's just a matter of time and effort.

My wife and I enjoy walking Kennesaw Mountain in Georgia. On clear mornings, we can see the Atlanta skyline far off in the distance. On other mornings, when we reach the top of the mountain, all we can see is thick fog. It's so dense that it's difficult to see anything beyond a few yards from where we're standing.

When it's foggy, it's almost hard to believe that the Atlanta skyline even exists. But our subconscious knows it does and tell us so. That's what faith is all about. Just because we can't see the skyline doesn't mean it's not there. It's always there. Accordingly, just because you can't *see* what's possible for you doesn't mean it's hopeless. Your possibilities are endless. They're waiting for you to reel them into reality. Just believe that they exist and take action on them!

Are you sitting on a great opportunity or a dream that's been stirring within? Are you still waiting for your life to begin? If you're waiting for everything to be right before you decide to take action, it'll never happen. After all my years in business, if I've learned anything, it's that things will never be "straight." As one motivational speaker said so eloquently, "You're either in a problem, just leaving a problem, or heading toward one."

There's always an excuse you could use to avoid moving forward today. But if you don't do it today, you could get distracted or lose momentum. My wife's grandmother always used to counsel her, "Baby, don't wait until everything is straight before you do somethin' because the only time things will be straight in your life is when you're lying straight out in that casket." Read these words of wisdom again and let them sink into your soul.

To exercise faith, you've got to do something. Merely talking about what you would like to do is not faith. Doing something when you don't know how, that's faith! Taking action on something when you don't know whether it will work out is a demonstration of faith. Faith gives us the fuel we need in order to continue on life's journey through not-so-pleasant experiences.

Claim Your Independence!

Why do we ask God to do what he's given us the power to do? I know many people who are just sitting down, waiting on God. They'll never reach their full potential because they've given their power away and refused to come out of their shell. The graveyards of the world are filled with people who have died with their dreams, gifts, and talents tightly locked inside of them. Though a parent, friend, or relative can be sincere in his or her so-called helping, there's a point where it's essential for them to let go. Be self-responsible in working things out more independently. How else can we learn to fly and leave the nest?

I believe in helping those in need. But refusing to let those we care about get the knocks they need in order to grow isn't helping them. It limits them from successfully living a life of independence. Those who never put much effort into making their own way because others always come to their "rescue" are being set up for a life of mediocrity.

I've listened to sad tales from hundreds of parents who have approached me after presentations. They wanted me to either talk to their kids or give them advice on how to get their children to, as my grandmother would say, "straighten up and fly right."

Many parents looked back with regret on how they reared their children—admitting they hadn't spent enough quality time with them or given them enough freedom to make their own mistakes. They also admitted they were overprotective when it came to allowing their children to experience some of life's pressures. The children did not have the opportunity to develop the fortitude and character needed to become successfully independent individuals. Now adults, they often lack the necessary tools to deal with the ups, downs, and uncertainties of everyday living. And of course, this only gets perpetuated to future generations.

Children who come from wealthy families often don't have the same drive and ambition that their parents used to build a business or career. They were not around to experience or were too young to understand their mother's or father's years of struggle to generate a good income. The children take everything for granted. The parents often become frustrated with them because of their "psychology of entitlement" attitude. The children may think that having the so-called niceties is their birthright. By the time parents realize they played a major role in their child's helplessness by doing for them what they could have done for themselves, it's too late to do anything about it. When you do everything for your child, dependency will be carried over into adulthood.

Somebody's Got to Stir the Nest!

David McNally, in his book, *Even Eagles Need a Push,* told the story of how the eagle, considered the prince of the air, still has to be pushed into greatness. Eagles don't soar through the air with confidence as soon as they emerge from the egg. Eventually, the mother has to "stir the nest." She has to make it so unbearable that the desire for the eaglet to leave the nest outweighs its desire to stay. But eagles like you aren't meant to stay in the nest; they're created to soar! Like eagles, people, too, sometimes need a push into greatness.

—3—

Service Is an Attitude, Not Just a Department!

"It's not what you do that matters, but how much love you do it with."
—Mother Teresa—

When times are challenging, serve more, not less. We all like to be served, and we all need to develop a liking for serving others. After all, serving others leads to success.

Think about it for a moment. Who works in every service department in the world? That's right, people—some who often have poor attitudes toward customers. They tend to sit around as if they are outdated, worn out furniture. Consequently, they cramp the style and hurt the entire organization. I once read that Mother Teresa would kindly tell her fellow Missionaries of Charity to stay home if they could not come to work every day—and take care of the hungry, homeless, and the sick—with a smile on their faces. She often said, "It's not what you do that matters, but how much love you do it with." Every organization has a unique culture, made up of the spirit of its people.

If you mention the word *service* to some people, they will probably equate it to being in a restaurant or any other place where *they* will be served. But what about *your* contribution? Are you service

33

oriented? Are you constantly on the lookout to find ways to better serve your supervisors, clients, customers, employees, associates, family, mate, or others? Do you even think about the service you give? Sadly, many would probably answer "no" to many of these questions. But as it says in the scriptures, "The greatest leader is the servant of all."

• What is it about "service" that automatically causes countless people to skimp? Maybe they don't know that the quality of their relationships, or the success of their business, is largely dependent upon how well they serve others.

Service really comes down to one thing—attitude. When you're at a hotel such as the Ritz Carlton, Westin, or Embassy Suites, and one of their staff members says, "My pleasure," after you have made a request, you know right away, just by their attitude, if it *really is* a pleasure.

Attitude influences everything! Think about this example: A human resources department is seriously considering three highly qualified candidates for a promotion. The manager happily tells the promotion panel that Stephanie, Melinda, and Louis are the leading candidates. Without a doubt, though, Melinda has the most experience.

During the meeting, someone on the panel announces, "Okay folks, we need to eliminate Melinda right now!" Everyone gasps.

"I know she has the most experience, but she's not service-oriented. I've heard far too many complaints about her lousy attitude, and it's difficult to work with her because she's not a team player. I'm tired of dealing with customer complaints regarding her poor service. Now tell me…who are those other candidates you were talking about?"

Welcome to the real world!

A bad attitude can negatively impact people for a long time. I was in a bank in Atlanta about fifteen years ago. I remember it as if it were yesterday—standing patiently in line, waiting to withdraw some money from my checking account. The young man who was standing in front of me slowly walked up to the counter. He quietly gave the bank teller the information she needed so he could make a withdrawal from his account. She quickly keyed the account number into the computer, read his current information on the screen, and loudly responded in a hot, scorching tone, "Sir, it would be IMPOSSIBLE for me to give you $20 out of your account when you only have $2.27 available!"

Needless to say, I felt sorry for the guy. I'm sure he wanted to crawl under the nearest rock. As a matter of fact, I would have crawled under it *for* him if I could have. If he becomes a millionaire one day, guess where he probably *won't* be taking his money?

A few years ago, I was doing business with another bank and just happened to go to a branch that had recently opened. As I pulled up to the drive-thru teller window, I noticed the young lady had a scowl on her face.

I asked, "What ever happened to service with a smile?"

She responded, "I did that last week at the grand opening."

Her reply was too ridiculous to address. Hopefully, the CEO doesn't condone such behavior.

It's never any fun dealing with organizations where I dread talking with the people. Life already has enough challenges. Just ask kids which teacher they enjoy the most, and I'll bet it will be the one with passion, enthusiasm, and an attitude of service. Students actually experience accelerated learning and retain more in a positive environment.

I remember doing business with a guy in Orange Park, Florida, who was extremely dedicated to pleasing his customers. His staff was very courteous and enthusiastic. In addition to running a quick oil-change business, he owned the car wash located next door. Customers could get their oil changed, fluids topped off, carpet vacuumed, and a complimentary air freshener for their car.

And that's not all....

The customers would also get a packet of Armor All for their dashboard or tires, a token for a free car wash, and a lollipop. After this incredible display of teamwork, you were out the door in ten minutes. Is that effective teamwork or what?

Now, it's time for a pop quiz. Write down everything you get with *your* oil change. How long does it take? After I moved to Atlanta in 1991, I found myself planning my trips back to Orange Park to visit family and friends around the time I needed my oil changed. When you take the time to go above and beyond the call of duty, people notice. It's also been proven that those who experience the joy of serving others are actually healthier.

Several years ago in November, I was visiting a nursing home in Orangeburg, South Carolina. I was going from room to room saying hello to the residents. Some of the residents couldn't see very well, and a few of them would yell out, "Junior, is that you?"

I would reply, "No ma'am, I'm Spark Plug, and I just stopped by to say hello to everyone."

I'll never forget the resident in the last room I visited on that chilly day. It was evident that she was sad and disappointed. So I sat and talked with her for a while. After we finished sharing a few bits and pieces of conversation, I was just about to leave when she slowly reached out her frail hand and made a gesture for me to come nearer to her. Holding my hand in hers, she whispered words I'll never forget, "Young man, I just want to say thank you for stopping by and visiting with me today because *you* are the only visitor I've had all year. Thank you."

Many people waste no time getting rid of everything old in their lives. Old shoes, old dresses, old suits, old cars, etc., are often thrown away and, sadly, some of us do the same with the elderly. We often forget to serve them by giving just a little of our time. Ralph Waldo Emerson wrote, "The *only* gift is a portion of thyself."

"Can You Teach Me How to *Act* Like I Care?"

When I worked in the health club business, it gave me great pleasure to assist my clients in building well-toned bodies. Some of them were bashful, first-time members, which required that I spend a little extra time familiarizing them with the equipment. Not only did I spend time giving them helpful workout tips, I also had to make a certain number of sales each week. So, between personal training and recruiting new members, I organized my time wisely and became one of the health club's top salespeople. Success didn't come because I was a great time manager. It came because my existing clients often gave me referrals in exchange for the exceptional customer service they received.

A new associate who had been studying my technique came into my office one day. He was one of those guys that the ladies raved about, a sort of Denzel Washington or Tom Cruise type. Mr. Cool, as we called him, never had any problems getting clients to sign up because most of the ladies flocked to him.

Anyway, one day, I was totally shocked when he stood in the doorway of my office and made a solemn request. "Spark Plug," he began, "I've been checking you out for the past couple of weeks and you're really a great salesman. You're so good with the people, you act as if you really care about your clients and they seem as if they really like you. I was wondering…can you teach me how to *act* like I care?"

I paused for a moment, looked at him in disbelief, and slowly answered, "I'm sorry, my friend, but that's not something I can teach you. It has to start inside. It can't be an act. It has to be genuine."

I noticed the look of disappointment on his face, despite trying to maintain his cool and calm demeanor, he looked rather shocked. It was not quite the answer he was expecting. My associate was only looking for a sales technique to use on his potential clients.

Although Mr. Cool was popular with the ladies, and could use his good looks and charisma to get the sale, he was clueless about service after the sale. Therefore, he was left with an extremely high cancellation rate and plenty of unhappy customers who were not interested in sending him any referrals. Because my clients knew I cared, they willingly made my job easier by giving me valuable referrals of roommates, coworkers, and others who eventually came to the club and signed up with me. Service is definitely an attitude, not just a department!

"**B**e ashamed to die unless you have won some victory for humanity!"

—Horace Mann

—4—

Commit—Plant Seeds That Can Yield Abundant Fruit

"If you're endeavoring to complete a worthy task without a strong commitment, it is equivalent to trying to eat soup with a toothpick or getting a giraffe to climb a tree."
—The Spark Plug—

Webster's dictionary defines commitment as "a pledge or promise to do something." But I like the candid definition that reads like this: Commitment means keeping your word even when the going gets tough. It's easy to keep our word when we are excited about something and things are going well. But what if our enthusiasm loses its spark? Do you fulfill the pledge or do you abandon ship just because things got tough? Too many of us are guilty of this.

There are rewards for keeping your word and following through. You will never know the positive impact you could have made on your life and the lives of others if you had kept your earlier promises and commitments.

Commitment Holds Things Together

When we promise or pledge to do something, it requires responsibility and accountability. Countless numbers of people excuse themselves from taking responsibility for their actions, and, unfortunately, they're often not held accountable. They lack commitment to their goals and do not strive for excellence. Frantically they're always in search of a loophole, and tend to give up when they think the pressures of life are overwhelming them. Most of their work often lies in an *unfinished* heap, while their dreams go up in smoke.

Imagine how our world would be if everyone refused to commit themselves to carrying out their daily tasks with integrity. The buildings in which we work would be so weak they'd probably collapse because the architects and builders didn't commit themselves to doing a quality job. Our clothing would be discarded after one use because of poor manufacturing. Our vehicles would have to be taken to the repair shop daily. Business deals would seldom be made, and sales would rarely take place.

Commitment is not always easy. It sometimes requires us to do things we no longer feel like doing. We sometimes have to deal with people with whom we would rather have no dealings at all. Even though lack of commitment abounds in society, you can still be known as someone who keeps your word. After all is said and done, our word and our relationships are all we have. Always act with integrity, treasure your relationships, and honor your agreements.

Think about the people you know whose word is as good as gold. When they say they'll do something or meet you somewhere, you never have to wonder if they will rise to the occasion. Wouldn't it be heartbreaking to know only a few people you can count on to keep their word? If you're thinking about making a commitment you have no intention of keeping—please save everyone the trouble by not lying to them.

Providence Demands Commitment—*Not Luck*

Commitment will bring rewards to us that are greater than we can ever imagine. I don't believe in pure luck when it comes to achieving goals and making dreams come true. It's not enough to help anyone succeed. However, there are millions of people in the world waiting for luck to come knocking at their door! Millions are also deluding themselves by looking to win the lottery. Lady Luck flashes her brilliant smile of untold treasures, plays the song of the siren, and weaves a web made only for those who are looking for a quick fix. Many die without working to achieve their goals, and their feeble attempts to live an abundant life turn to ashes.

One of the few things I remember about my grandfather was he always told us, "Once my lucky number comes up, I'm going to do all kinds of nice things for y'all."

With glee, we would all jump up and down and holler, "Really, Grandpa, really?"

He would reply, "That's right, kids; once I hit that number."

Well, you probably already know the ending. His lucky number never came up. He was never able to do all the nice things he had promised because he died before his number rolled around.

At any rate, "Thanks for the hope, Grandpa."

Don't be like my grandfather and dream about your number coming up. Direct your energy toward something more rewarding. Putting all of your hope in a pie-in-the-sky pipe dream that disappoints millions of people each week will rob you of more than a few dollars.

Sure, there are times when people receive things they didn't really earn or stumble upon opportunities without seeking them. But luck is one of those words or ideas that often lures others into a world of expecting something for nothing. The most unfortunate people are those who came to this earth, grew old, and left without leaving a trace. They never took the time to positively nourish someone else's life or stand up for their dreams. It was the distinguished Horace Mann who cried out, "Be ashamed to die unless you have won some victory for humanity!" Are you doing anything to leave the world a little better than it was before you got here? Concentrate on being a shining light in your corner of the world.

Total commitment is planting a seed or idea, nurturing it, and being steadfast until your goal or dream is achieved. It means faithfully weathering the hardships of life because you know brighter days lie ahead.

Providence does not begin to move until *you* begin to move. From the very moment you exercise your commitment, start looking forward to small miracles that inspire you to keep moving toward your goal.

Nothing Can Stand in the Way of Commitment—*Not Even a Near-Fatal Accident*

In the summer of 1993, I started my first business in advertising and publishing. All of my efforts were centered on providing affordable advertising to traditional small business owners on a community-by-community basis. Just when I was halfway finished with my second business directory, I was involved in a near-fatal traffic accident.

A car was stalled in the middle of the highway, which I failed to see until the last second. The two cars ahead of me quickly darted to the left and right lanes, narrowly missing the broken-down car in front of them. However, I wasn't as fortunate. Traveling at sixty miles per hour, I slammed into the back of the stalled vehicle on Interstate 285 in Atlanta, Georgia. Immediately, I was knocked unconscious.

It is only in the fires of life that we have an opportunity to measure our dedication and commitment to our work, family, dreams, and goals. This was definitely one of my *fires* of life. I was forced to reflect on my favorite James Allen quote that says, "Circumstance does not make the man, it reveals him to himself."

My car was a total loss. It was crushed and crumpled as if it had been made of aluminum foil. The driver's side door had to be ripped from its hinges in order to free me. I was stuck behind the wheel like a Sumo wrestler pinned to a canvas.

After the paramedics skillfully removed me from the car, I was immediately rushed by ambulance to the hospital. I suffered a cut on the top of my head, a lacerated lip, and had severe internal pain. While at the hospital, I discovered that a truck had smashed into the rear of my car—knocking me off the road. I felt as if I had been run over by a herd of angry cattle. Even though I was in a lot of pain, they discharged me later that day.

The accident made the local television news that evening. It was a miracle that I survived.

Before the accident, I was a one-man show, operating my business on a tight budget. Every penny of my savings had gone into starting and marketing the business. It never occurred to me that everything would literally come to a screeching halt. I was completely helpless for three long, agonizing weeks. I had no income and of course, there were bills that needed to be paid. I had no transportation, no relatives in town, and the insurance companies were refusing to pay for damages. But I was still committed to getting my publication out on time, at any cost.

While lying in bed in excruciating pain for three weeks, I didn't focus on having a pessimistic attitude. I did not wallow in self-pity and ask, "God, why did you let this happen to me?" I was optimistic. I asked myself questions like, "How can I get out of this situation and turn this whole thing around? How can I overcome this calamity?" Since I was still alive, I had just enough faith to believe that everything would work out for the good, regardless of the state of my physical condition.

My brother came up from Savannah to visit me and offered to loan me some money. After paying some bills, once again, my checking account was almost running on empty. I had a big decision to make. Either pay my rent with the little money I had left or put the money down on a used car so I could have some transportation to get rolling again.

I decided to buy the car and vowed to work extremely hard the next week to earn the money I needed to pay the rent. The following Monday, my first day back at work, I made three big sales. I was determined to honor my word to my clients. Two months later, I successfully completed and distributed my second publication on time. I was committed to my goal and dedicated to the people I served.

Get Serious!

A lack of commitment has led to termination from promising jobs, thwarted the building of businesses, destroyed families, broken marriages, alienated children, ravaged communities, ruined relationships, and the list goes on. If you want to make a name for yourself, let it be one that people can look to and say, "There stands someone who is committed to doing what he says he will do." A great philosopher wrote, "One single pursuit is the easiest road to success." Putting your heart and soul into one single idea can actually help you accomplish a great deal and provide more substance, depth, and creativity to your work. Whatever you decide to do, be a hundred percent committed.

Do Your Best and—*Move On*

I remember what I consider the worst speaking engagement of my life. In 1994, I planned and scheduled my very first public seminar, *Overcoming Your Fears*. Jacqueline, my wife, who was my fiancée at the time, told me not to memorize my speech word for word because I might get on stage and forget what I was supposed to say. But I was stubborn and didn't listen. I wanted to do things my way. I quickly replied, "I can do it. I'll do just fine."

She simply said, "Okay."

On the evening of the seminar, after a local radio personality had given me an award-winning introduction, I dashed onto the stage. I was ready to dazzle the audience with a power-packed presentation.

Suddenly, I couldn't remember a thing. All I could see were bright lights shining in my face. Beyond the blinding lights was only a sea of darkness. I couldn't see anything or anyone past the first two rows. Things had gotten so bad, I couldn't even remember my name, much less the speech I thought I had carefully folded and tucked away in my mind.

I moaned to myself, "Surely this couldn't be happening to me, I know this speech like the back of my hand!"

Everything was a blur.

Perspiration was rolling down my face like raindrops on a window. My heart was literally beating out of control—thump-thump, thump-thump. I was drowning in humiliation. I tried to scan the first two rows to find Jacqueline. I needed to somehow get a glimpse of someone familiar, or maybe uncover a shred of hope by seeing her reassuring face. But the lights were too blindingly bright. I struggled to present my speech even though I had done it countless times before—at home, in the car, and even in the checkout line at the grocery store. But I couldn't do it.

My mouth was dry and I wanted to desperately crawl off the stage and run for cover. The wrath of dead silence in the huge auditorium was tormenting me, and I could feel a multitude of glistening eyes glaring at me through the darkness. I was considering the idea of obeying the thundering voice in my head that bellowed, "Get off the stage, just walk off...you're making a complete fool of yourself...just who do you think you are anyway?" Then, suddenly, ever so slowly, the information began to filter into my mind so that I was able to share it with the audience. I couldn't believe it. I was actually beginning to utter words that made sense and was able to share *Overcoming Your Fears* straight from my heart. The empowering words of Emmet Fox became a reality for me—"Do it trembling if you must, but do it!"

Evidently, I must have done a fairly good job, although I knew I could do better. After the speech, people came up and thanked me for what they thought was an outstanding presentation. Surprisingly, a young woman who heard me speak that evening called me a year and a half later. She thanked me again for a wonderful presentation and for the information I had provided on that memorable evening. Unfortunately, I didn't find out until years later that the success of any presentation is 7 percent words, and 93 percent body language. Even though I had forgotten the words to the presentation that night, I was sincere and my body language was positive.

Get Back in and—*Do It Again*

Jacqueline and I knew that my presentation was missing a spark. Frankly, when I was practicing, I thought I could have won an award for Speaker of the Year. But after that lukewarm speech, I had a big knot in my stomach; I was disappointed with my performance. I told myself that the other motivational speakers could have the speaking business all to themselves. I didn't want to stand up on a lonely stage ever again, staring into a sea of darkness for the rest of my life. Yet in my heart of hearts, I knew I had a positive message to share with others that was bubbling over and could not be contained. Life would not let me rest until I recommitted myself to becoming a professional speaker.

One week later, my friend, Lisa Jones, extended an invitation for me to give the keynote address for 850 students at Camp Creek Middle School. It was the largest group I had ever spoken to up until that time. Finally, I was able to redeem myself by giving a great presentation. I had learned my lesson the hard way. Memorizing a speech word-for-word would always be number one on my speaker's list of things *not* to do. It may work for others, but not for me.

I didn't think I had enough skills to be a part of an international speaking organization. But since I had made a commitment to become a public speaker, I had to master the basics. I also had to feel the fear and do it anyway as Dr. Susan Jeffers wrote in her book, titled with those words. After joining the speaking organization, I found that it was exactly what I needed for encouragement and to nurture my dream. It allowed me to be with people who were where I wanted to be. I eventually spoke at more than fifty local speakers' clubs around the metro Atlanta area, and thanks to commitment, I became one of the most sought after speakers in the organization.

Since that humbling experience on stage many years ago, being committed has enabled me to travel and inspire people in organizations around the country.

So often, many of us start a task and then put it aside after we become frustrated. But keeping on is one of the keys to success.

Commitment is necessary. Falling on your face is required. Determination is essential. Embarrassment is inevitable.

If you're endeavoring to complete a worthy task without a strong commitment, it is equivalent to trying to eat soup with a toothpick or getting a giraffe to climb a tree. So go back and get that idea, build that business, go to that seminar, or whatever it was you laid aside. Dust it off and give it another go.

Until you've given it all you've got, you can't honestly say you've done your best. You'll always wonder if you would have succeeded had you stuck it out. Don't spend your entire life wondering—get busy. The world is waiting for you to do it! Whatever you would like to do, wherever you would like to go, or whatever you would like to become, be committed to its fruition.

Make a commitment to yourself that you will be known for something you have literally poured your heart into, whether it's being a speaker, parent, teacher, writer, manager, scientist, musician, plumber, carpenter, tennis player, computer guru, or business owner. Become known for having a commitment to excellence in all you do. Andrew Carnegie boldly stated, "The average person puts only 25 percent of his energy and ability into his work. The world takes off its hat to those who put in more than 50 percent of their capacity, and stands on its head for those few and far between souls who devote 100 percent."

"**W**hether they appear to be or not, everyone is hurting to one degree or another. Treat people like they're hurting and you'll be treating them right.

—The Spark Plug

—5—

Celebrate Life and Make Peace with Yourself!

"Look well into thyself: there is a source of strength which will always spring up if thou always look there."
—Marcus Aurelius—

Not only does a celebration of your life involve the miracle of your birth, it also includes the fascinating journey you are on. You are not here by accident. You are truly a masterpiece, a beautifully written song, a blazing star in the night, poetry in motion, and a gift for all seasons!

The pattern for your unique skills, abilities, knowledge, contributions, and talents was delicately written in your mother's womb. Imagine being a blueprint even before your physical self arrived. Amazing, isn't it? Nature's stage hands pulled back yet another royal silk curtain when you made your grand entrance.

Nature wasn't concerned about your looks or what colors you liked. It wasn't concerned about whether you would like spinach or had the ability to sing like a songbird. When you came out kicking and screaming, nature understood another human being had won the privilege of breathing air. Nature also understood that there were gifts and talents deposited in you that you could share with the world. A sacred appointment was set for you to arrive on this earth and, now, here *you* are, reading a book that was a part of *my* blueprint in my mother's womb.

Since we're here, it's imperative that we treat ourselves and others well. But if you don't appreciate and make peace with yourself, it's almost impossible to wish the best for someone else. If you don't pour healthy love upon yourself, it is very unlikely that you will freely pour love upon your children or other people around you.

I recently read an article in *USA Today* about the benefits of taking care of yourself. A successful college professor admitted he started treating himself better after he had bypass surgery. He now craves travel to exotic places—including an around the world cruise he has promised his wife.

Don't wait for something drastic to happen before you heap healthy love upon yourself. Treat yourself well because you deserve it.

Nobody Knows How Much My Heart Hurts

Whether they appear to be or not, everyone is hurting to one degree or another. Treat people like they're hurting and you'll be treating them right. When hearts are hurting, people may not comprehend the depth, breadth, and intensity of the gnawing pain they, perhaps unknowingly, inflict upon others. But they can't reduce their own pain by inflicting pain on others; that would only make things worse. Their silent screams for help can be manifested as a whip that unmercifully beats upon the feelings and emotions of the people around them. The real tragedy is that, all too often, some of them also turn on *themselves*. The Center for Disease Control in Atlanta has reported that more people die from suicide than from homicide. Overall, suicide is the eleventh leading cause of death for all Americans, and is the third leading cause of death for young people between the ages of fifteen and twenty-four. It has been documented that every fifteen minutes, a person commits suicide in the United States alone.

Though every situation is different, I am convinced that many who commit suicide often despise themselves so deeply that they can no longer coexist with the person they have imagined themselves to be. They no longer find life meaningful and have literally become suspended in an *awful* world, which they perceive to be lonely, cold, wicked, and meaningless. They feel as if they have lost control of everything, and they just want the pain to stop. Internal emotional collapse eventually causes them to rid themselves of themselves. Material goods are not enough to mend the torn fabric of their broken lives and wounded souls. Many of them constantly tell themselves the following:

> I am inadequate. I am stupid. My parents are ashamed of me. I never get anything right. I'll never be able to do thus and so. I am worthless. I am so lonely. I wish I could have lived my life another way. Nobody cares about me. I can't lose this weight. My mother abandoned me. Everybody is always picking on me. Everyone is out to destroy me. Why did my dad or mother leave me and why won't he or she ever call? I'll never be able to get out of this financial mess. Why is this happening to me?

Unfortunately, unhappiness is a common state of mind for many people. Fatalistic thoughts seem to constantly hover over the sad souls who snuff out their lives. They lose all hope and submerge themselves in a pit of worthlessness. More often than not, they can hear only the blaring voices of those who belittle, not the powerful words of encouragement that are so rare. Somehow, they have managed to convince themselves that their world is the only one that is crashing into smithereens. In *Anatomy of Melancholy,* first published in 1621, Robert Burton said, "If there be a hell upon earth, it is to be found in a melancholy man's heart."

Depressing? Sure. However, the reality of this situation remains the same. Way too many people slosh around in this negative pool far too often.

None of us have all the answers. None of us are perfect nor will we ever experience a perfect life on this earth. Perfection is a myth, a moving target. Many of us are constantly in search of something or someone who will make us complete and keep us content. But somehow, the search always seems to lead us right back to ourselves. It has been said, "If you cannot find peace within yourself, you will never find it anywhere else."

Our greatest desire is to be free on the inside. We want the security of knowing that someone genuinely loves us as we are. Sometimes an entire lifetime is required to work out the kinks that cause us to become internally bound.

Sadly enough, the suicide survivors, those who are left behind, suffer tremendously. They are left with no real closure, no real answers, and no relief. Just as they struggle with the guilt of not having been able to identify someone else's pain, they also wallow in the guilt of not having been able to get through to a human heart that was hurting so much.

But Don't Lose Sight...

Because our vision is so limited, we will never know how the story of our life will end. If we don't stay until the curtain falls, we just might miss a powerful and awesome scene. You never really know how things will work themselves out. The happiness we are capable of experiencing is even greater when we make it through our share of sorrow and pain. It doesn't matter how much pain lives inside of us, there still resides a reservoir of strength. Marcus Aurelius proclaimed, "Look well into thyself: there is a source of strength which will always spring up if thou always look there."

We often underestimate the needs and the value of just being human. We forget we are connected in ways we cannot imagine. We need each other in order to survive. We are all companions riding along in the same vehicle, spaceship Earth. Everyone cries out for a little civility in some form or fashion. Research has proven that babies can die if they aren't held enough. We desperately need the transference of unconditional love and concern from one to another. Unfortunately, it is only during times of tragedy that many of us can get a glimpse of this phenomenon of how much we really need each other.

Lady Bird Johnson noted, "It's odd that you can get so anesthetized by your pain or your own problem that you don't quite fully share the hell of someone close to you." The real issue of suicide often lies in being totally consumed with *self,* i.e., your wants, your needs, your problems, your pain, your shortcomings, or your disappointments. Work with those who could use your help. It has an interesting way of changing your perspective and trivializing everything that ails you.

Remember, no matter what the circumstances may be in your life, it's never too late. You can always pick up the pieces of your dream and complete your assignment. Every day is a crisp new page in the storybook of your life. What memories will you write on the pages of your existence today? Whatever you've experienced or whatever decisions you've made, they are all wrapped up in your destiny to be great. Nothing is ever wasted. Life will gladly be your number one tutor in spite of the choices you've made. In spite of the pain that was inflicted upon you, something of value can still be extracted from every challenge.

Dear God—*I Don't Wanna Be Me*

I heard one of my favorite speakers admit that in all of his many years of teaching, when his students were asked if they could be anyone in the world, who would they choose…the majority always chose someone else. He went on to say, "The hardest battle you're ever going to fight is the battle to be just you." Few of us are satisfied with the physical qualities, talents, and gifts that we have.

Do you often find yourself envying the traits and attributes of someone else? Time and time again, do you say to yourself, "If only I had this or that, or if I had made this decision or that decision, I would be at such and such a place just like so and so?" In fact, you couldn't be further from the truth as life makes no guarantees. Since our life spins us in so many different directions and weaves such an array of experiences for us, it would be foolish to say that we will all end up in the same place if we all made the same decisions. There are just too many variables and influences that would prove this theory wrong. Nevertheless, where we are in life does not define who we are, just as our past does not determine our future.

Maybe you feel as though you've somehow missed out on an opportunity because you had to make certain sacrifices at the time. Or maybe you berate yourself for not making the "right" decision. But as Ralph Waldo Emerson wrote "For everything you have missed, you gained something else." It's difficult to appreciate what we've gained if we concentrate only on what we *think* we've lost.

Unfortunately, we will always sell ourselves short when we compare our lives to others. Without question, comparing ourselves to others is a *serious* problem. It causes us to live far below our potential, forces us to live a cookie-cutter life, and convinces us that we must behave as if we belong to a herd rather than celebrate our individuality. Our imagination and creativity are often snuffed out because we spend so much of our time imitating what the masses are doing. The obsession for instant gratification, that is, buying things we can't yet afford, perhaps to impress others or to imitate celebrities, can often take center stage in our lives. This may overshadow the person we were destined to be, and interfere with the contribution we were sent here to make.

Equally oppressing is the fact that many people believe it is imperative that they surgically change their outward appearance even when there seems to be nothing physically wrong with them. Some believe that by changing the outer appearance, a magical change will occur inside that will take them into the stratosphere of self-acceptance and acceptance by others. On the contrary, some doctors counsel patients not to expect a life-changing experience after a face-lift or other physical enhancement surgeries. They're encouraged to begin a journey on the inside that will help them accept who they are and love what they already have—in a world that constantly says we're not good enough.

Suppose you didn't like your *new* face or *new* nose. What then? Will you subject yourself to the knife again and again? Not only is the risk of going under the knife potentially life threatening, but there is also a chance of permanent disfigurement.

Surgically changing outward appearances can be just as addictive as food, drugs, or gambling. I am in no way criticizing those who choose to enhance their features, but I want to remind you that the authentic side of you begins on the inside and shines on the outside. If we live long enough, the time will come when gravity wins the war and steals our youthful features forever. The life we have nurtured on the inside will be our only hope for having days of true contentment.

"The only people who will tell you it cannot be done are the people who have never accomplished anything in their lives! Those who have had some success know that anything is possible, and the last thing they want to do is extinguish the flame of hope in others."

—Lou Holtz

—6—

Develop an Attitude of Fortitude!

*"Fortitude is the marshal of thought, the armor of
the will, and the fort of reason."*
—Francis Bacon—

Let's face it, anyone who has done anything out of the ordinary knows that unexpected things happen when we finally make up our mind to follow our dream. Obstacles seem to appear out of nowhere. Sometimes they may irritate us and hinder our efforts to move forward. When we work our way through them, we may wonder if we made the right decision to step out of our so-called comfort zone. The decision to move forward always brings a challenge, an uphill battle, because anything worth doing comes with a price. The bigger the challenge, the greater the effort—and the greater the reward. So, get ready for the ride of your life!

Great achievement requires persistence. Develop an attitude of fortitude that enables you to get back up no matter how many times you fall. The dictionary defines fortitude as, "that strength or firmness of mind which enables a person to encounter danger with coolness and courage, or to bear pain and adversity without murmuring, depression, or despondency; courage; resolute endurance."

As the ancient Chinese proverb advises, "If you get knocked down seven times, get up eight." It took ten years after its invention until the airplane was taken seriously. Many religious pundits claimed that if God had wanted man to fly, he would have given us wings. The clock was not refined with the first design, neither was the television, fax, cell phone, computer, CD, or DVD. Nothing great was ever achieved on the first attempt. The trial-and-error method is as normal as the sun rising in the east. Because of our instant gratification culture, many have the notion that we must succeed the first time we do anything. But the results we want require more than a few attempts, testing our commitment.

It's Okay to Fumble

Ahhh, mistakes—the hooded creatures that can haunt us and eat away at our confidence. "You made a mistake. Shame on you," society screams. "Mistakes are taboo, a no-no!" They are the embarrassing acts that cause us to shy away from the things we really want in life. For some people, it takes years to gather up the courage to go at it again. Others have the Jack-in-the-box approach and *pop* back up in no time at all. They understand that mistakes can be the key that opens the door to enormous success. Effective leaders have been known to encourage their people to make mistakes on a regular basis.

When we risk and make mistakes, we have an opportunity to learn more. We will make more contributions to any organization we're associated with than those who are afraid to take risks. Tom Watson, the founder of IBM, made it a point of telling people, "If you want to be successful, increase your failure rate." As William James proclaimed, "It is only by risking that we live at all." Each time we set out to do something new, we learn something new.

You're going to make mistakes; you're going to look foolish at times; and people may even laugh at you. But in the end, their laughter will mean nothing because you'll be one step closer to what you truly want. Just as life keeps moving on, so will you. Don't let a temporary setback keep you down. One of my favorite quotes of all time is, "You're not a failure if you don't make it; you're a success because you made an effort." I can't remember who said this but I'm sure glad they did.

I remember the first time I used this particular quote in a speech. After the presentation, a woman came up to me in tears. I asked her what was wrong and she sobbed, "Thank you for that quote. For years I thought I was a failure until I heard you say, "You're not a failure if you don't make it, you're a success because you made an effort." She went on to tell me the story about how she had lost $80,000 in the stock market. Her self-confidence went bust, and this poor lady thought she was a failure because she picked the wrong stock and lost her money. After she heard me recite that quote, she said she felt as though a heavy burden had been lifted from her shoulders. She confirmed that words are powerful and have the power to *change* lives.

PUSH—*Persist Until Something Happens*

What do all great people have in common? They have an attitude of fortitude that enables them to persist against the odds. They developed a dogged determination to persist until they succeeded. No matter what happened, they stayed focused on their goals and were not distracted by the "good" opinions of other people.

Sylvester Stallone understood what an attitude of fortitude is all about. At one of the many high schools he attended—he was kicked out of several—he was voted "most likely to end up in the electric chair." Sylvester was even homeless at one time during the early years of his acting career. He found himself sleeping in a bus terminal with other homeless people. Even after numerous rejections from Hollywood producers for his first film, *Rocky,* he never gave up. One producer said he would finance the movie only if an established actor starred in the lead role. Stallone refused. He firmly believed he was the only person who could bring *Rocky* to life on the big screen.

He was told on several occasions that the movie was corny and would never be a box office success. Yet, *Rocky* delighted fans all over the world with its story of hope, determination, and triumph. It received an Academy Award for Best Picture of the year. In Philadelphia, where the movie was filmed, there's even a statue of the *Rocky* character. Since I am an avid *Rocky* fan, I am pleased to say that *Rocky VI* is being made a reality. Fortitude definitely pays.

My mother told me about a gentleman whom she had the pleasure of hearing speak at a seminar in Tulsa, Oklahoma. His name was Peter J. Daniels. Mr. Daniels told his incredible story of how he failed every grade when he was in school. Now, he's a world-recognized authority on leadership, personal development, and goal setting. He has also served on boards in numerous countries. What's so amazing about his towering achievement is that Peter was virtually illiterate at twenty-six years old.

He shared his heartfelt story about his grade school teacher, Miss Phillips. She told him emphatically, "Peter Daniels, you are a bad, bad, boy and you are never going to amount to anything!" Many who have encountered a Miss Phillips in their own lives may have given up, but Peter was determined to prove her wrong. He wrote a book as a *lesson* to his teacher titled, *Miss Phillips, You Were Wrong*. His attitude of fortitude was the key that unlocked the door to achievement.

A few years ago, I was participating in a celebrity charity event for ACDelco RapidFire spark plugs. I was making an appearance on behalf of the company as their Human Spark Plug with Hank Aaron, major league baseball's all-time homerun king. When I met Mr. Aaron, I asked him how he was able to break Babe Ruth's long-standing homerun record—in spite of the criticism, death threats, and media frenzy that surrounded the homerun race. I wanted to know how he was able to withstand so much pressure and take so much heat. I'll never forget what he shared with me face to face on that cool winter day.

He began, "Spark Plug, let me tell you something; I was extremely focused in my pursuit. I was also *determined* to break that record. I wasn't going to let anyone or anything take my mind off my goal! It was one of those things that I just *had* to do and *nothing* was going to stop me." His passion and sheer determination reminded me of something Ferdinand Foch, Supreme Commander of the Allied Armies during WWI, declared, "The most powerful weapon on earth is the human soul on fire!"

Hank Aaron did what many great people do. He made a decision and was steadfast in his commitment to see it through until it was accomplished. He didn't let his emotions cloud his vision. He didn't let the threats of strangers frighten him away from what he wanted to achieve. He didn't heed the chilling voices of those who wanted him to retreat. Hank kept chipping away at the rocky mountain until it became a pebble. Hank Aaron's attitude of fortitude enabled him to persist and reach his goal.

Read biographies about people who succeeded in spite of the obstacles they faced. You'll be ignited with inspiration to continue your journey. Read about the lives of people you admire. Their achievements will give you a dose of encouragement and hope for your future.

I like what Francis Baron wrote regarding fortitude. Let his words of wisdom inspire you to keep pressing on: "Fortitude is the marshal of thought, the armor of the will, and the fort of reason."

A lack of fortitude can cause you to miss your calling and forfeit everything you've longed to be. I had the honor of meeting Og Mandino, the prolific bestselling author, one month before he passed away. He encouraged his readers in his classic book, *The Greatest Salesmen in the World,* to "persist until you succeed." There are many who have marvelous ideas but they are not persistent about moving the idea from the intangible to the tangible. They give up before their ideas are moved from thought to reality. Until you have the tenacity to keep pushing and pushing, your ideas will never come to fruition. Sometimes an idea gets stuck somewhere between excitement and taking action. Someone advised, "Don't ask God to guide your footsteps unless you are willing to move your feet." It might help if you made a list of the top five things you need to do in order to get started and then, get started. Master one task at a time. Then move on to the next.

Now Where'd You Get that Crazy Idea?

When it comes to your ideas, guard them well. Beware of the faithless; the friends you thought would cheer you on. Don't be surprised if they're also the ones who ask, "Where did you get that crazy idea?" They may even try to label you as foolish. If they do, you'll know you're on to something!

Ted Turner experienced this when he first shared his idea, with friends and media experts, for a twenty-four hour news station. One expert commented that the idea wouldn't be economically feasible. Another so-called expert told Ted he would be out of business in six months. This expert also went on to say that CNN should stand for *Chicken Noodle Network* because you would have to have noodles for brains to think this hair-brained idea could ever work.

Even though Ted didn't know much about the news business, he believed the time was ripe for a twenty-four hour news station that broadcasted not only national news, but international news as well. Today, CNN is the premier twenty-four hour news station in the world. It is where many of the world's leaders go to get their news and information.

Refuse to let others hang around just to sprinkle doubt on your ideas and aspirations. If you give them an opportunity to put a wet blanket on your enthusiasm, chances are they will. More often than not, they don't mean much by it, it is primarily their own fear of doing the impossible, which speaks on their behalf. In essence, they don't believe they are capable of doing something great or worthwhile. Since they have this *mistaken* certainty for themselves, they try to impart this faulty belief system onto others who may aspire to do great things.

Regrettably, they speak from a level of awareness which is different than yours. As the old saying goes, some people see a glass half empty, while others see it half full. They are afraid; they try to cast their fear upon you and anyone else who will listen.

When I attended the 1998 National Speakers Association Convention in Anaheim, California, Lou Holtz, former head football coach of Notre Dame (he hadn't yet taken the job with the University of South Carolina), was one of the speakers I had the honor of hearing. He emphasized something that really struck a chord with me and has stuck with me after all these years: "The only people who will tell you it cannot be done are the people who have never accomplished anything in their lives!" He went on to say that, "Those who have had some success know that *anything is possible*, and the last thing they want to do is extinguish the flame of hope in others."

Even though you may be caught up in your own excitement about your dreams it isn't wise to share them with everyone. Treat your ideas and dreams as something sacred because they are. Find people who will support you, or you'll have to operate solely on your own inner strength.

Recently, I spoke with a friend who has temporarily abandoned his dream, because, unfortunately, everyone he shared it with said something negative about it. He told me I was the only one who had anything positive to say. But with only one positive and so many negatives, they have won, and he has lost...for now. However, I encouraged him to give it another go; but this time—just do it! I advised him to develop an attitude of fortitude and not tell anyone else about his idea until it was accomplished!

"Thoughts shape our lives. They are the seeds that will either inspire us with ambition or hold us back. They are the judge and the jury when it comes to making decisions. They can either lead us to the brink of death or guide us toward vibrant health, peace, happiness, love, and prosperity."

—The Spark Plug

—7—

Thoughts—The Gateway to Our Future

"If we don't control our thoughts, our mind will be controlled by outside forces, which are usually negative."
—The Spark Plug—

Thoughts shape our lives. They are the seeds that will either inspire us with ambition or hold us back. They are the judge and the jury when it comes to making decisions for our lives. They can either lead us to the brink of death or guide us toward vibrant health, peace, happiness, love, and prosperity. They can cause us to feel like a prince or a princess in an opulent palace or a pauper behind prison walls. Iron bars are not always required to confine a prisoner. It is typically our own thoughts that create barriers to a better quality of life for ourselves as well as our families.

Are your thoughts helping you to do your very best or are they tearing your inner being to shreds? Are they encouraging you to pursue your dreams, vision, or purpose, or holding you back? Did they destroy your feelings of self-worth? Are you constantly preoccupied with what other people think about you? How often do you entertain self-defeating thoughts of yesteryear or even yesterday?

Don't live your life based on what happened in the past. Leave it back there where it belongs. If we have regrets and could change it, we would. But since we can't, why would we want to keep beating ourselves up over it? Constantly focusing on what happened back then will only serve as an excuse for not enjoying the present, and will cast shadows of limitations on our future success.

Our thought life is the most difficult area of our lives to tame. If we would constantly focus our thoughts on the good of humanity and ourselves, how drastically different everything else would seem. I am not suggesting that our thoughts have the power to single-handedly change everything. However, they determine all of our actions, thereby creating positive or negative results in our lives.

We think at the rate of approximately 1300 words a minute and speak at a rate of 150-250 words a minute. What other people say to us is far less important than what we say to ourselves. It's been said that over 80 percent of our self-talk is negative. Is it any wonder why many people look so frustrated? They become impatient, irritable, and on edge, leading to lack of success in all areas of their lives.

Would you like a better quality of life? If so, the change begins with a positive thought life. As we've so often heard, the real battleground is in our own mind. If we don't control our thoughts, our mind will be controlled by outside forces, which are usually negative.

Marketing gurus Al Ries and Jack Trout write about how companies are in a battle for our minds as consumers. The marketplace is flooded with subtle influences that sway us to make certain decisions. Advertisers have figured out how to make up our minds for us. If we are constantly fighting with ourselves internally, pet rocks and other useless items are easier to sell.

Fighting for Forgiveness

Our whole world suffers from a lack of forgiveness. Generations upon generations carry around this seed of unforgiveness that is potent with anger, strife, jealousy, and prejudice. For many, the tranquil sea of forgiveness is dry and barren, but the bloody sea of unforgiveness is filled to the brim and running over. Everywhere we go, it's as if we're dragging along a heavy, weather-beaten suitcase, packed with dirty, unresolved issues. They often block our progress, dampen our spirits, and sometimes send us spiraling into a dungeon of depression and despair.

To jumpstart your heart, put pep in your step, and add life to your years, forgiveness is necessary. It has been found to be the cure of the ages. Its positive electrical current can reach clear across the ocean. It won't cost a cent and it will give you freedom you never dreamed possible. Though it may be tough at times, practice forgiveness on a daily basis. If you want peace in your life, you must forgive. To shut and lock the door to a painful past, forgiveness is the key. Forgiveness is difficult because it requires that we give, lay something down, or cast something aside.

Forgiveness is a healing ointment. It can also be an antidote for any hurt or pain. If we allow it to perform its task, it will hasten the recovery of the deepest wound. We will immediately feel better and our vision will once again be clear. Our life will be less stressful as we exercise the gift of forgiveness.

Hospitals are packed with people suffering from various illnesses. However, a percentage of them are suffering because they simply need to forgive someone. Many times, doctors are puzzled after they have administered every test imaginable and are still unable to find the cause of a patient's pain. These phantom illnesses are caused by an emotional or spiritual infection aggravated by unforgiveness. It then manifests itself in the form of physical pain, which may lead to sickness. Unfortunately, physicians are unable to use a scalpel or prescribe medicine that will heal these types of illnesses—only forgiveness will.

Release Them—*Let Them Go*

There is an unrelenting howl from some in society to become hardened, bitter, cold, and intolerant. Many of us give in to it, while others fight to overcome its monstrous negativity. Nevertheless, the call is continuous. We may feel powerful when we refuse to forgive others but, in reality, it is a manifestation of weakness. Gandhi said,

"The weak can never forgive. Forgiveness is the attribute of the strong."

How long must we let our friends, acquaintances, and family members dangle on the "rusty nail" of unforgiveness? How long will we use unforgiveness as a means of keeping them in shackles? Letting them off the rusty nail is not for them; it's for our own peace of mind, health, prosperity, and happiness. We need to forgive for ourselves. There are no benefits in unforgiveness. The only results we'll receive are: the inability to fully enjoy the gift of life, ten years added to our face, a heavy burden on our heart, fragmented relationships, and phantom physical ailments.

To embrace the present, the past must forever remain in the past. Forgiveness begins when you are strong, noble, and willing enough to let it all go. It is an act of humility. If you are interested in destroying your future, let your mind dwell in the swamp of the past. Let your decisions and actions have their roots firmly planted in the soil of yesterday. If your creative energy is directed toward revenge, you will never experience the freedom that comes from forgiving.

We don't always feel that forgiveness should be extended to those who have caused us sorrow or pain. The wound is often so deep that we wonder if we will ever recuperate. Everywhere we look, we are reminded of the pain. There is no strength left in us to forgive. All we can feel is grief. But dealing with the pain of grief is one of the seeds for growth and healing. You've *got* to feel the pain. If you ignore or deny it, you will remain in bondage and hinder yourself from experiencing strong, fruitful relationships.

Grieving is healthy. Go ahead and grieve. Grieve a little more. And grieve some more if you need to. Then...*move on.*

I took a giant step toward healing when I forgave my father for not participating in my life. He wasn't around to give me tips on how to live a successful and productive life. He never took me fishing. He never taught me how to drive. He never taught me about the responsibilities of being a man. He never saw me compete at any of my tennis tournaments. He probably never knew I became good enough at tennis to play at the college level. He wasn't there to give me helpful hints on shaving, dating, or any other aspects of life. He didn't even see me graduate from high school or college.

When I was young, I often heard my friends rave about their relationships with their fathers. I lamented over the fact that I never saw mine. Why couldn't I have a dad at home? Why didn't he love my sister, brother, and me enough to call to make sure we were even still alive? Did he even care at all?

Sure, I still think about him and feel the icy stab in my heart... every now and then. But I came to a place in my life where I *needed* to forgive him. Hanging on to my anger toward him was interfering with my progress, personally and professionally. I had to release him. I had to let him go. I had to forgive him so I could be emotionally free to live my life to the fullest. I didn't excuse him for ignoring that I was his younger son, but I forgave him for the years of pain and suffering his negligence had caused.

The people you need to forgive may never change. They may never acknowledge how they have mistreated you or how they neglected their responsibilities. You may never feel that your mother or father really loves you, but it's still imperative, for your own well-being, that you release them. For your own sake, for your own sanity, for your own future, *let it go*. Love yourself enough to do it!

When we let forgiveness flood our soul, we experience peace. We are freer to love ourselves and others more. We are no longer bogged down by the excess baggage, and we can experience a bright new beginning. The real problem does not lie in being unable to forgive but merely refusing to do so. To pick up the armor of love, we must lay down the burden of hate. Forgiveness is simple, sometimes tough, but always necessary.

Release Yourself Too!

Releasing yourself from hanging on the same rusty nail means dealing with the residue that guilt and shame have left behind. It must be dealt with in order to experience healing. Guilt and shame are not lovely gifts that you need to keep around. Even if someone attempts to place the burden of guilt upon your back, you don't need to accept it. People from your past will constantly remind you of your mistakes and faults, but you're the only one who can put yourself on the altar of forgiveness and stay there. Start with loving, forgiving, and respecting yourself. Then you can pass the torch of love, respect, and forgiveness on to others. As the ancient African proverb says, "If there are no enemies within, the enemies without can do you no harm."

Worry Whittles Your Life Away

Peter Daniels defined worry as "Creating mental pictures of the things you do not want." Even though worry is unproductive, many people spend a vast majority of their precious time swimming in it. All day long, we are creating movies in our mind—our own little secret place, filled with either pessimism or optimism.

A wise person said, "Worry does not empty tomorrow of its sorrow; it empties today of its strength." Most of what we worry about will never come to pass. When I started my first business, I constantly worried about going out of business and it never happened. Today, that business is almost fifteen years old.

The media does a great job of instilling fear. "Fear this; fear that; don't eat this; don't eat that; don't go here; don't go there; don't buy this; and don't buy that." People literally become frozen in fear. Television, newspapers, magazines, the Internet, and radio bombard us with so much negative information that it could cause many to barricade themselves in their homes. As a citizen of the world, I want to know what's going on in other parts of the world, and if it's important enough surely someone will tell me. There's always some positive news out there somewhere. But what's even better than that is to make our own positive news, and be a positive example to others!

The media promotes fear and insecurity, which encourages many people to distrust others. The media also wants us to believe that we can purchase items that will keep our homes and material possessions safe. Consumer-attracting motivation is often what's behind over-concern in preparing for a challenge that never shows up.

In reality, no one pays much attention to the screeching sound of an activated car alarm system anymore. It was reported in the national news that California police departments are considering *not* responding to home alarm systems at all because they've found that over 90 percent of the alarms are false anyway. Some police departments actually fine people if they are called out because of a false alarm! What does this say about our society? I'll let you consider that one for yourself.

Some people don't even lock the doors to their homes. Why? They believe that if you lock the doors to your home, you are really imprisoning *yourself.*

Go Jessica—*Go!*

Negative thoughts seem to come to us more often than positive ones, but we don't have to pull out a chair and ask them to stay a while. I think the writer Terry McMillan was right on target when she wrote: "Too many of us are hung up on what we don't have, can't have, or won't ever have. We spend too much energy being down, when we could use that same energy—if not less—doing some of the things we really want to do."

I was watching a news program one night when I saw an incredible story about Jessica Parks, a seventeen-year-old high school student who was born with no arms. Her story was so inspiring that I sat staring at the television in awe of this remarkable young lady. She had an unbreakable spirit and a great attitude about life. Instead of looking for pity from others, she inspires them with hope. Jessica said there wasn't too much that was hard for her growing up. "I just learned to adapt and had my parents and my friends to help me on my way."

Jessica was a member of the National Honor Society and an athlete on her school's soccer team. She also drove the family tractor that had five gears and a sluggish steering wheel. Her next goal was to learn how to drive a car. This would require special equipment to help her steer with her feet.

The most amazing thing I saw Jessica doing on the show that night was putting her contact lenses in her eyes, *by using her toes!* When we see people like Jessica doing the so-called impossible on a daily basis, we know deep down in our souls that we could be doing more with our lives rather than sitting in a pool of worry. The words of Dorothy Galyean constantly remind us that "Worry is like a rocking chair—it gives you something to do but it doesn't get you anywhere."

—8—

Get on the Road to Your Destiny!

"My mother always told me when I was a little girl that the most handicapped person in the world is a negative thinker, so for me, being deaf was never a handicap when it came to accomplishing my goal."
—Heather Whitestone McCallum—

When I was in the health club business, my friend and fellow sales associate, Cecil Morris, shared something with me about character that's worth repeating.

We had been talking about self-improvement when he said, "Spark Plug, it really doesn't matter how much positive material a person reads or how often they attempt to apply spiritual principles. If they don't have a foundation of character, what good is it?" Character is something we would like to assume most people have—at least those we *think* we know. It was something I never really took the time to think about, but Cecil's point made perfect sense.

Positive reading materials and time-tested principles have no power to help us change or improve our lives, if we don't have enough character to implement what we learn. What is character anyway? Webster defines character as—moral strength: self-discipline, fortitude. When character is missing in our lives, it leaves a gaping hole in everything we do. Most people will sense dishonesty in us if we lack character. Many will see that we are not who we claim to be. We are merely *masquerading* as someone who has integrity.

The moral fiber of our society has been stretched thinner than fiber optic cable. Over the last few years, the media has reported countless stories about corporate leaders who have acted as if they were above the law. They displayed a severe lack of character. Many of those leaders have even robbed their own employees of company stock options, retirement funds and, worst of all, destroyed trust in the corporate world. With all of this corruption going on, is it any wonder why some people have just given up on society?

Whatever you do and whatever kind of life you lead, you can be sure someone is watching to see if your actions are in line with who you say you are. If someone promises to do something for me and I share that with someone who's relying on me, my ability to keep my promise relies heavily on the first person. If they fail to keep their word, it usually prevents me from keeping mine. In other words, if they don't do what they said they would do, then I can't always do what I need to do. It's as simple as that. Always keep your word. If you change your mind, you need to discuss the possibility of modifying the original agreement.

I Want a Winning Team

Think back to when you were in school. Do you remember your physical education classes? When it was time to choose team members, we only wanted those we believed could help our team win. Right? We didn't want classmates who didn't give a hundred percent. We wanted those on our team who had the same goal in mind—winning!

Well, what happens to the desire to choose a winning team when it comes to winning in life? People, young and old, have a tendency to absorb the pessimistic mannerisms and attitudes of those they associate with, like a sponge absorbs water. To remain focused on fulfilling your purpose or destiny, you must constantly be aware of the company you keep and how they are affecting you.

My profession would be very difficult for me if my wife denounced everything I did or criticized the suggestions I had for the business. On the other hand, her part in it would also be tough if I was critical of her actions and suggestions. We couldn't possibly make any real progress if we were weighing each other down with negativity. But because of our love and respect for each other, we are usually able to agree on an idea and act on it quickly. It makes the journey easier and the load much lighter when there is support in your corner. I've found that people are typically doing one of three things:

- *Building you up*—"You can do it! I know you can because you've got what it takes."
- *Tearing you down*—"You're too stupid to learn anything new. You're too old to go back to school. That idea will never work."
- *Saying they don't have time for you*—"Oh, I got your message; I just didn't get around to calling you back. I've been too busy for lunch."

Place yourself in the company of visionaries—people who sincerely want to make a difference in the world. Just being in their company will help you think bigger. And if you listen more than you talk when you're in the presence of these visionaries, you may even discover some new strengths and abilities in yourself that you never knew you had. If you don't think you know any visionaries right now, make a list of your friends and associates who are passionate and excited about life. Find a productive way to spend more time with them rather than hanging around negative people. This is where you'll get most of your encouragement and support. It's something we all need.

We're All Born with a Measure of Greatness

Gilbert Young, the world-renowned artist, is a good friend of mine. While at lunch one afternoon, he shared a story with me about his childhood. Gilbert told me that when he was in elementary school, a teacher labeled him a slow learner. He was then placed in a special education program. When Gilbert was in the sixth grade, another teacher came along who really believed in him as well as in his artistic abilities. This teacher encouraged his mother to enroll him in a free program at the local art academy, which she did, and he had immediate success.

Gilbert attended a vocational high school, and upon graduation, won an astounding forty-seven Key Awards in the arts. He also received a full scholarship to the Cincinnati Art Academy. Gilbert started competing and exhibiting in art shows at the age of nineteen. In the U.S. Army, he served as the battalion's artist.

Years later, this so-called slow learner impressed his family and friends when he became curator of the University of Cincinnati's Fine Arts Collection, which is known to be worth millions. Today, his works of art are featured in galleries around the world. Gilbert Young's world famous painting, *He Ain't Heavy* has sold nearly one million prints.

There will always be people who will want to place a negative label on you or tell you what you cannot do. Ignore them and keep going!

Heather Whitestone McCallum's mother didn't listen and because of this, in 1995, Heather became the first deaf Miss America in the pageant's seventy-year history. While in Valley Forge, Pennsylvania, speaking for a telecommunications company, I had the pleasure of having lunch with Heather, who was also one of the featured speakers at the conference.

As I sat across the table from her, I said to myself, "Who knew? Who knew that a little deaf girl from Alabama, who endured six grueling years of speech therapy just to learn how to say her last name, would one day grow up and become an inspiration to the world?"

When asked how she was able to accomplish her goal of becoming Miss America, Heather replied, "My mother always told me when I was a little girl that the most handicapped person in the world is a negative thinker, so for me, being deaf was never a handicap when it came to accomplishing my goal."

Heather's mother created an environment of victory around her daughter rather than an environment of defeat. Gilbert's sixth grade teacher was the catalyst that changed his life and paved the way to a future filled with creativity. We need to create a winning team around us if we truly want to accomplish our goals and achieve great things.

We can all create a winning team for ourselves by joining a positive organization. Do whatever it takes to contribute to its success and inspire others along the way.

If you don't already have one in place, join a support group of associates who get together once or twice a month to encourage and support one another. If some are unable to meet on a regular basis, send cards, letters, emails or make phone calls to stay in touch, and offer your assistance to help them grow. Most importantly, create a winning team.

"...You Never Know Who You're Talking To"

I heard Jim Rohn, a fellow professional speaker and a titan in the business, say, "Always remember, you never know who you're talking to." He was referring to the fact that most everyone hasn't made it to where they are going. Some people may be down and out today, but sailing on the sea of prosperity tomorrow. You just never know.

In 1993, George Andrews was trying to find investors for his new bank idea. He was having a very difficult time securing the necessary funding. During this period, I spoke with George on several occasions. Though he was a little frustrated at times, because things were progressing so slowly, he was still very excited about the big picture.

To make a long story short, ten years later, George became President and Chief Executive Officer of Capitol City Bank & Trust, which now has six locations around the metro Atlanta area.

At the grand opening celebration of his first bank, a local radio station had a live remote broadcast in the parking lot. One radio personality spoke with a gentleman who had grown up in the same neighborhood as George. This gentleman told a story about a little elderly lady who predicted great things for George when he was a youngster. She used to warn some of the kids in the neighborhood that they shouldn't pick on little George because he was going to grow up and do something great one day. George is a perfect example of, "You never know who you're talking to."

The most uncertain thing about life is, we don't know what the future holds for us nor do we know whose hand we will need to help us along the way. So whether we feel like it or not, we need to spread a little sunshine wherever we go.

You're an Ambassador!

When I was in the United States Navy, I was assigned to the USS Dwight D. Eisenhower. This aircraft carrier weighed 95,000 tons. It could hold up to 100 airplanes and well over 6,000 sailors. The ship was literally a small town out on the sea. Whenever we pulled into a foreign port, our captain could be heard on the ship's 1MC (public address system) making this announcement: "Hello gents, (At that time, women were not on board aircraft carriers.) this is the captain speaking. Before we pull into port today, I just want to remind you that you are Ambassadors of the United States of America. So please, conduct yourselves accordingly."

The commanding sound of his voice was so captivating, it would virtually stop me in my tracks. It could cause almost anyone to pop to attention and listen up. The captain's words really made me feel important, as though I was a part of something special. I remember how good it felt the first time the captain told us we were ambassadors. I said to myself, "Can you believe that? I'm an ambassador!" I knew the word ambassador meant, a special representative and as U.S. military servicemen, that's what we were. As I strolled around the ship with my head held high and shoulders pulled back, I said to myself, "I'm an ambassador!"

After we pulled into the port of Toulon, France, I had the opportunity to ski the French Alps at the Isola 2000 resort. It seemed as though it took traveling all day on our tour bus to get to the resort. I remember going up, and up, and up the mountain for about three or four hours before we finally reached the top. Once we got there, the one thing that stands out the most in my mind, even today, is how pleasant and hospitable all of the resort staff personnel were. Everyone, from upper management to the grounds crew, offered his or her daily, "Bonjour, Monsieur." We had the best time skiing the French Alps!

Around lunchtime, I asked my friends, with whom I had been skiing all morning, if they were ready to go to lunch.

They all declined. "No, man, the powder (snow) is too thick and we're having too much fun. You go ahead and we'll catch up with you later," one of them said.

As I sat on the restaurant deck eating lunch, I watched the other skiers having a great time in their brightly colored and uniquely designed skiwear.

The attractive young lady sitting next to me struck up a conversation. "So, where are you from?" she inquired.

"The United States," I responded.

"Wow, America!" she exclaimed.

"What about you?" I inquired.

"Oh, I'm from London, England," she gracefully replied. "What do you do?" she politely asked.

I thought about the words our captain had spoken and as I squared my shoulders a little, I diplomatically replied, "I'm... an...ambassador."

"An ambassador! That's great," she excitedly remarked.

By this time, one of her friends had walked up to join us at our table.

She boasted to her friend, "He's an ambassador, isn't that cool?" Her friend seemed very pleased with my *perceived* importance.

"Well, what kind of ambassador?" her friend wanted to know.

I paused for a moment to get my thoughts together. Then smiling to myself, I quickly replied, "I'm a Goodwill Ambassador from the United States, and I'm pleased to meet you!"

They were both elated. My captain had taught me well. That statement, alone, reminded me that I not only had the duty of positively representing the United States Navy, but I also represented my fellow citizens. No matter where we go or what we do, we are still a representative of our wives, husbands, children, mothers, fathers, sisters, brothers, grandparents, and our organizations.

Our decisions never affect us alone. There will always be other people who will feel the impact of the choices we make. There will also be those who will have to pick up the pieces of our carelessness. The people we surround ourselves with will either keep us on the road to greatness, keep us mired in the mud of mediocrity, or lead us down a trail of destruction. The choice is ours.

—9—

Who Sells?

"Commissioned sales reps and business owners choose to live in the realm of possibilities, and typically earn the highest of incomes."
—The Spark Plug—

When we understand that everyone sells, we will view sales professionals in a more positive light. By now, some of you are probably saying, "Spark Plug, what do you mean by that?" Simply this: We're all selling something.

One of the best books ever written about the sales profession is *How to Master the Art of Selling,* by Tom Hopkins. When it comes to sales, this book is definitely on my top ten list as a must read. In this book, Tom states quite emphatically, "Nothing takes place unless a sale is made."

When you meet with your boss to ask for a raise, it's in your best interest to be confident and know how to *sell* yourself and your accomplishments. *Sell* your skills and your personality when interviewing for a job. When someone is expanding a business, he or she *sells* the idea to a prospect. Even when you're interested in capturing someone's heart, you often spend a great deal of time *selling* him or her on your wonderful attributes. Whether it is an idea, automobile, a bar of soap, personality, jumbo jet, or a million thumbtacks, no transaction will take place unless a sale is made.

Sell...Sell...Sell!

If you took a public poll, I have no doubt that you would find most people *prefer* a guaranteed weekly, biweekly, or monthly income. The thought of being on 100 percent commission is enough to send most people scampering for something they describe as "a little more sure and secure." But where's the adventure in that? Commissioned sales reps and business owners choose to live in the realm of possibilities, and typically earn the highest of incomes. This forces them to understand the real meaning of going forward in *faith*. When you have the right market, meet and present to enough qualified people, have a great attitude, know and believe in your product, service, or opportunity, and have a little patience and the persistence to keep going, you can be a winner in business.

When I met Jacqueline, she was working with one of her friends who owned a retail shop. Because she wasn't selling much merchandise, she became disenchanted with her job. After she expressed her frustration to me, I shared a book with her titled *The Greatest Salesman in the World,* by Og Mandino. After reading this inspiring book, published in 1968, she learned sales is a profession she was taking much too lightly. She began realizing that selling is an art.

Within a few weeks after reading the book, her sales more than doubled simply by applying the principles she had learned. She also gained a new level of self-confidence and greater respect for successful salespeople. Her greatest reward was that she became more excited about her work and looked forward to improving her sales record every day.

Joe Salesman—*That's My Name*

Once upon a time, I worked for a thriving California-based sign company that had a branch office in Atlanta. It specialized in custom-made outdoor signs that would give traditional retail businesses optimum advertising exposure. Our three-day training session ended with all of the recently hired employees traveling to Savannah, Georgia, for some *real-life* training in the field.

When the time arrived to exercise my newly acquired skills in selling outdoor signs, my first stop was to be Tybee Island, a sleepy little town about thirty miles south of Savannah. I was quite excited about driving down to find out whether I could really interest someone in buying a new sign. Tybee would be my testing ground.

After scouting around Tybee looking for potential customers, I stopped at a nearby lawn mower repair shop to see if I could sell the owner a new sign. From the looks of his current sign, it seemed to me as if Mr. Lawn Mower Repair was long overdue for a change in his company's image. As I entered the shop, I carefully stepped over a few broken-down lawn mowers.

When I finally reached the owner's office, I found him sitting at his desk writing out a check to a young lady from the local Chamber of Commerce.

I knew he'd either be in a buying mood or tell me to get lost. Since I really needed the money at the time, I hoped and prayed he'd want to buy. We exchanged greetings and made a little small talk. He was one of the many friendly people I encountered on that bright, sunny day in the cozy beach town of Tybee Island. When we had finished chitchatting, I made my presentation. When I was finished, I nervously asked for the sale.

Mr. Lawn Mower Repair immediately began to exhibit some trepidation about buying the sign. He started ranting and raving about the fact that I had to have his check that day, made out in my name, which would be his deposit for the new sign. On top of that, I also had to go to his bank to cash his check and get a money order or cashier's check made out in my name. This wasn't something I magically pulled out of thin air just because I was in desperate need of the money. This was the company policy we had been instructed to follow at the three-day training session.

Mr. Lawn Mower Repair was not happy with this arrangement. He began a deliberate cross-examination of me.

"Let me get this straight! You're selling signs in Tybee Island today. The company you work for is in California. You're from Atlanta and you're training in Savannah. You have a Florida tag on your car, and you want me to write this check out to you so you can go across the street to my bank and cash it, and then get a cashier's check in your name! Are you kidding?" he asked incredulously.

I was amazed at how well he had listened, observed, and then put all of the pieces together, and in order. At that point, I paused for a moment, looked him directly in the eye and calmly agreed, "Yes sir, that's exactly what I want you to do."

To my surprise, he picked up his checkbook and asked, "Now, how do you spell your name?"

I walked out of his business with a smile on my face and his check in my briefcase. My prayer had been answered. I'm glad Mr. Lawn Mower Repair trusted his instincts and believed in me.

About a year or so ago, my wife and I were in Tybee Island. As we passed by the expanded Mr. Lawn Mower Repair business, I noticed that the sign I had sold him over twelve years ago was still providing his business with optimum advertising exposure. I was reminded of the day I had walked into his office and made that un-forgettable sale—and it felt good that I had made a difference.

As far back as I can remember, I've been a salesman. I've always had sales in my blood. As I mentioned earlier, we're all selling something. My earliest recollection of sales success came when I was in the seventh grade at St. Andrews Junior High School in Co-lumbia, South Carolina. That year, I entered a selling competition at school. The top prize was to go to the student who sold the most na-tional magazines. I decided to sell the magazines door-to-door in my neighborhood.

At the end of the contest, to my amazement, I discovered that I had sold more magazines than any other student. Because of my success, I won a stereo and some other prizes. The following year, when I was in the eighth grade, I, once again, outsold all of the stu-dents who competed in the contest. This time I won a trip to Carowinds, an amusement park located on the North Carolina/South Carolina border.

In high school, when it came to talking my way out of trouble, I was the best. One day, I was sent to the assistant principal's office for eating candy in class. After the assistant principal, Mr. Cannon, threatened to send me home for a few days, I had to act as my own defense attorney to keep him from doing so.

When I had finally convinced him to see things my way, he confessed, "Young man, you have the gift of *persuasion.*" He then added, "Hopefully, one day you will use your unique ability to persuade others in a positive manner."

I've always been a talker. I always thought I had something to say. Upon graduation from Columbia High, I went off to Newberry College in Newberry, South Carolina. Being at Newberry gave me another chance to test my sales skills. Even though I had never been in student government in high school, I sold myself to the freshman class as their best candidate and was nominated class president. I did my best to run a personable campaign and was blessed by a landslide win. I cared about the people. Believe it or not, I was a little shy so campaigning forced me to meet new people. I enjoyed shaking hands, mingling with the students in the freshman class.

"Could You Use a Good Bargain Today?"

After Newberry College, I moved to Atlanta. Since I had a passion for face-to-face selling, I went to work for a company that allowed me to sell pots and pans, stereos, crystal wine sets, steak knife sets, plates, pool sticks, and any other knick-knack you could possibly think of, from the trunk of my car. This really tested my tolerance for pain, but it helped me develop inner strength. There were days I ate only after I had made a sale, which sometimes didn't come until late afternoon or evening. It was more important for me to sell than to eat!

I'll never forget my job as a traveling salesman. I'd drive through the states of Georgia, South Carolina, and Tennessee, hollering out to potential customers from behind the wheel of my car, "Hey, ma'am!" or "Hey, sir! Could you use a good bargain today?" I'm sure some of those people thought I was crazy, a real loony on the loose. But I had sales to make and a quota to meet. I was a man on a mission. Some people didn't hesitate to tell me, "Beat it" or "Go take a hike." I was called all sorts of names I'd like to forget. Nevertheless, I understood some of their trepidation. On the other hand, many of the people I met were very hospitable and agreed to look at the items I had for sale. It was a very humbling experience and I'm eternally grateful for it. I learned a great deal about humanity, and I learned how to speak with confidence—to anyone, anywhere, anytime.

My next job was at Athletic Attic. I was the top salesman of the month several times and ranked among the nation's top salespeople. By the time I was promoted to store manager, our owner had bought his way out of the Athletic Attic franchise and changed the name to Sports A' Foot. Because of my energy and enthusiasm, the president of the company, John Smith, often referred to me as "Spark Plug." It seemed to be a perfect match for my personality.

I was very excited about being promoted to store manager. This new responsibility required me to attend the yearly managers' meetings in Colorado—a beautiful place that's truly reflected in the breathtaking postcards you may have seen. The majestic snow-capped mountains are spectacular! Thanks to a few ski lessons, I was able to ski down the Black Diamond Trail at Copper Mountain.

I Served My Country and Loved Every Minute of It!

After being with Sports A' Foot for two years, I joined the U.S Navy to serve my country and broaden my experiences. Traveling to destinations such as France, Italy, Africa, Mexico, South America, England, Spain, Turkey, Israel, and Monte Carlo really helped me gain a new perspective on life, and gave me a greater awareness and appreciation for different cultures.

I had a chance to visit the Sistine Chapel and the Coliseum in Rome. I marveled at the Leaning Tower of Pisa, and toured the island of Capri and many other spectacular cites in Italy.

In London, I had an opportunity to see the historic Big Ben clock and visit Buckingham Palace.

In Cannes, France, I attended the exciting Cannes Film Festival.

In Monte Carlo, I visited the Royal Palace and its magnificent gardens. I also paid my respects to the late Princess Grace Kelly by visiting her gravesite.

I had the opportunity to cruise through the Straits of Gibraltar and the Suez Canal.

I stood at the Wailing Wall in Jerusalem.

I had a wonderful time in the downtown area of Tel Aviv, and had some delicious spaghetti in Haifa, Israel.

In South America, I visited Caracas, Venezuela's capital, and the beautiful island of Margarita.

I played tennis at the Sporting Tennis Playa Resort on the beach in Palma, Spain. I enjoyed the challenge of negotiating for my goods with the vendors in Tijuana, Mexico.

My travels expanded my worldview, making history come alive. My love for reading further deepened while I was on two six-month cruises.

Between cruises, I became a Big Brother with Big Brothers/Big Sisters of Jacksonville, Florida. My little brother, Ishmael, was only twelve at the time, but now he's over thirty! Time really does fly. He's married with four kids and I still keep in contact with him and his family.

During my last year in the Navy, I found myself right in the middle of the Red Sea as a part of Operation Desert Shield. My ship, the USS Dwight D. Eisenhower, was in its fifth month of a six-month deployment when Iraq invaded Kuwait. We made it back to the United States only two weeks behind schedule and docked in Norfolk, Virginia at Pier 11. Thousands of happy family members, and friends of the military, greeted us with cheers and banners, welcoming us back home.

After visiting so many other countries, I developed a deeper appreciation for life and the opportunity we have to make a difference. There are wonderful people everywhere in this world of ours. We need to reach out to them and share what we have to offer.

"**A**fter hearing this message day in and day out for about two weeks, a funny think happened. We slowly started believing that maybe we could...."

—The Spark Plug

—10—

Tap into the Awesome
Power of Believing

"Obviously, the facts weren't going to help us reach our goal.
Believing was the answer."
—The Spark Plug—

It was 1991. After five years of serving my country, my first job back in the civilian world was working at a local health club, SportsLife, in Atlanta, selling memberships. Unfortunately, before too long, the challenge began fading like the sunset, and I started thinking about leaving the organization. But it just so happened that our general manager had been demoted and transferred to another one of our locations. Since the new general manager was known as the best salesman in the company's history, I decided to stay so I could learn from a real pro.

Our sales had been down at the club for a few months, and the company was steadily losing market share to our two biggest competitors. We *had* to do something quickly! It was clear we needed fresh leadership. The locations previously run by the new general manager never failed to reach their quotas while he was at the helm. He had no intentions of doing any less at our location.

I remember the first time he called a staff meeting. Standing in front of us, using his best Vince Lombardi impression, he shouted,

"Folks, I'm going to tell you up-front, you're not going to like me. As a matter of fact, you're going to hate me. But on the tenth and the twenty-fifth of every month (our pay days), you're going to love me because you'll be making more money than you've ever made in your lives!"

At this point, he had our attention, which was exactly what he wanted before he made his next announcement. He informed us that we would have three meetings a day, one in the morning, one in the afternoon, and a third one in the evening. But the next thing he said really blew us away. It was a wake-up call for all of us.

"...We Will Hit Quota!"

He continued, "I also want each and every one of you to know that we *will* hit quota!" We all looked at each other as if to say, "Quota...what quota? We have a quota? No one has ever said anything to us about a quota!"

Not only did we find out that we had a quota to meet, there was also the added pressure of knowing that our new quota for December was about $150,000! Our past general manager was a very laid-back kind of guy and had never set any quotas. We all just went with the flow and did what we thought was a good job. Our new general manager surely had his work cut out for him.

At each of our three daily meetings, he shouted the same mantra repeatedly, "We will hit quota! We will hit quota!" After hearing this message day in and day out for about two weeks, a funny thing started to happen. We slowly started *believing* that maybe we could hit quota.

Our new general manager's prophecy quickly came to pass. I wouldn't say we hated him, but he wasn't one of our favorite people either. He was also right about our paying homage to him on payday. As a result of being more disciplined and focused in our work, our paychecks grew enormously.

As the weeks rolled by, he continued shouting at every meeting, "We will hit quota! I don't care how you do it. Whether it's your mother, father, roommate, shipmate, sister, brother, or friend that you sign up, I don't care," he yelled. "Don't figure out how you can't; figure out how you can!" Having someone around with this much passion and belief in our abilities was a totally new concept and experience for us.

Finally, we all began to feel the pinch because our time was running out. There were only three days left in December, and we were about $40,000 away from our goal. He called us into his office and gave us one of his pep talks about not giving up, as he, once again, quoted the great Vince Lombardi. My associates and I looked at each other as if to say, "This guy really believes we can hit quota."

He refused to be counted out. He was pounding on his desk, bellowing, "We will hit quota, we will hit quota!" His leadership style wasn't pretty but it was effective.

I left his office saying to myself, "Yes, indeed, we can hit quota. If he really believes it, I guess we can." From that day forward, my fellow associates and I were determined to hit quota.

Well, the last day of the year was going to be a shorter workday than usual. Since it was New Year's Eve, instead of opening at 6 a.m. and closing at 10 p.m., we opened at 8 a.m. and closed at 4 p.m. The general manager called us into his office one last time on that memorable morning and told us that we had to sell $20,000 in memberships in order to reach our goal.

In the back of my mind I was saying to myself, "I've never seen this club do that much business in one day." However, at that point, we couldn't rely on the facts. Obviously, the facts weren't going to help us reach our goal. Believing was the answer.

I'll never forget that day. We didn't just *hit quota* for the month of December; we surpassed it. Why? Because our leader inspired us to rethink what we thought was possible for ourselves. By the close of business on that momentous day, we had sold over $25,000 in memberships, continuing our boss's stellar track record. Our little club, the so-called stepchild of the franchise, with no pool or basketball court, got the job done. Even though our club was the oldest and certainly not the most glamorous, that day we outperformed all our other health clubs in the metro-Atlanta area! My friend, Cecil Morris, even sold a membership to his roommate.

Our general manager ordered pizza for everybody, and we had a little party to celebrate. That was one of the most exhilarating feelings of teamwork that I had ever experienced. In the end, we all refused to lose; we chose to work as a winning-together team, and we exceeded quota! But success would not have been attained if our general manager had not instilled the awesome *power of believing* in his team. As a wise man said, "Nothing splendid has ever been achieved except by those who dared and believed something inside them was greater than the circumstances."

—11—

Lead, Follow, or Get Out of the Way!

*"Effective leaders encourage their people to
believe in doing the impossible."*
—The Spark Plug—

When I was in the organization leadership program at Mercer University, I learned that leadership isn't about ordering people around; leadership is about inspiring them. Unfortunately, this aspect of leadership is what's missing in most organizations as well as in most families.

What does leadership mean to you? My philosophy of leadership is quite simple. A leader's first job is to inspire and encourage his or her people to believe in the impossible and strive for excellence. A leader also needs to be a big thinker and a visionary. He or she needs to know the organization's big picture, stay on track with it, and encourage their people to do so. Promoting the goal and vision of the organization only once or twice a year is ineffective and inadequate. A real leader promotes constantly.

Leadership is about being a solution to the problem, not a continuation of it. We're all affected by leadership or lack of it. Leaders are central to identifying potential in their people and helping them turn it into reality.

Effective leaders have the power to help others improve their lives. I've read countless definitions of leadership in my studies, but the one definition that always seems to stay on my mind is one I read in a Dubrin leadership textbook: "Leadership is the ability to inspire confidence and support among the people who are needed to achieve organizational goals." For me, the word that stands out the most in this definition is "inspire," which literally means to *breathe life* into something. When leaders truly understand the power behind this word, it can *transform* their organizations. Leadership is most effective when it is an organizational trait practiced by a group of individuals with the same vision.

Is There a Leader in the House?

We all have the potential to become leaders, but to do so we need to stop being just followers. Take the leadership challenge—accept the responsibility that comes with carrying the mantle of leadership. Some people may be born with a natural inclination to lead, but the vast majority need to *develop* their leadership skills. Frances Hesselbein, president of the Drucker Foundation, responding to the question, "Are leaders born?" stated, "I think few leaders are born; we learn to be leaders. We learn by working with other people and working through our own philosophy."

Many people have leadership traits but this alone is not enough and may not always lead to effective leadership. Self-confidence, enthusiasm, trustworthiness, passion, integrity combined with action, discipline, and a strong desire to lead are required to produce effective leadership.

Coach Eddie Robinson, one of the most successful college football coaches in the National Collegiate Athletic Association history, said this regarding effective leadership: "Leaders should always tell their people the truth." Of course, this needs to be done with a caring attitude. While this is not always easy, in the end you'll have the satisfaction of knowing that you did your best to do the right thing.

Leaders need to empower their people, promote diversity and teamwork, and inspire a shared vision—on a daily basis. They also need to be enthusiastic about the success of others, operate a mentor/mentee system, be the chief cheerleader as well as the coach, learn what motivates their people, and be an inspirational figure.

Inspiration—*The Breath of Life*

Let's get back to inspiration. Why is it so important? As Emerson said, "Our chief want in life is someone who will inspire us to be all that we can be." When you inspire your people to grow and excel through their challenges and they respond by doing so, sooner or later, you and your people will reach your organizational goals. We all need inspiration, especially during tough times. People *want* inspiration. When they get it, they have the go-power to accomplish amazing feats and achieve extraordinary things. One inspired person can make a difference, and change the world by leading others in the cause!

Richard Williams, the famous father and tennis coach of Venus and Serena Williams, knew the power of inspiration. He realized that his first job was to inspire his two little girls to be great! As Peter Daniels remarked, "What makes the great, great? It's a sense of destiny." Richard Williams *knew* that his two little girls were destined to do great things. So, back in 1993, he announced to the tennis world and anyone else who would listen that his two little girls from Compton, California, would one day be the number one and number two ranked professional women tennis players in the world. He also said they would be the proud holders of many Grand Slam championships. Guess what? The so-called experts thought he was a lunatic! They claimed this would never happen.

"Great tennis players don't come from Compton, California," the experts pointed out.

Well, Richard's prophecy came to pass. Serena and Venus eventually held the number one and number two ranked positions, worldwide, among female professional tennis players. Currently, they have twelve Grand Slam Singles tennis titles between them. Incredible!

Most effective leaders understand that they must do whatever they can to inspire their people. If you have to use metaphors, analogies, or anecdotes, do it. If you have to go in through the *out* door, do it!

Bill Gates is always on the lookout for ways to inspire his people. Lately he's been doing it by promoting his most recent vision for Microsoft Corp. Most of us remember Bill's vision for Microsoft in the late 1970s—to have a computer in every home. His newest vision for Microsoft is to "give people the power to do anything they want, anywhere they want, and on any device."

Bill understands that inspiring others is an *essential* leadership practice. When people are inspired, they feel better about themselves. They feel as though they are part of something worthwhile. Deep down inside, isn't that what we all want? The beautiful thing about being a leader is that we have the opportunity to create this kind of environment in our own organizations.

Leaders need to be inspirational figures at all levels of the organization—from the stockroom to the boardroom. In today's brutally competitive global marketplace, top-down leadership is not enough to sustain an organization in the 21st Century. Organizations need all team members to take a leadership role so they can be more effective in day-to-day activities.

Susan Drake made this point clear when she wrote about John Q. Hammonds, the legendary hotel developer, in her book, *They Call Him John Q;* "When he needs an answer, forget hierarchy and chain of command. John Q prefers to talk directly to the people who already know what he needs to know, and he actively seeks contact with people *throughout* his organization."

The Greatest Servant Shall Be the Leader of All

I was on the phone with a young lady from one of our favorite vegetarian restaurants in Atlanta. My wife and I had been dining at the restaurant one night to celebrate a special occasion. We had experienced a minor inconvenience that we wanted to bring to the owner's attention. So, when I called the next day to speak with her, the young lady who answered the telephone told me the owner wasn't available.

She inquired, "May I be of assistance?"

Again, I informed her that I would rather speak with the owner.

She then replied, "Sir, I am not the owner, but I try to conduct myself as if I own the place. I would really be happy to assist you."

And she did. This is exactly the kind of servant leadership that is needed to help organizations excel in today's extremely competitive marketplace.

Attention All Leaders—*Please Walk This Way*

When times are tough, we need to lead the way, not manage the way. Leaders want to grow beyond the status quo. Effective leaders make an effort to squash the "business-as-usual" mentality. They promote "business unusual."

As I look back over my life, I now realize that I worked for very few *true* leaders. Most of them were positional leaders. I had many managers but the true leaders were few and far between.

Unfortunately, many of us mistake positional leadership for true leadership. The two are not to be confused. The positional leader is recognized only because of his or her position in the organization. But true leadership doesn't require a position.

How many bosses have you worked for who knew absolutely nothing about leadership? This seems to happen quite frequently, especially in the sales arena. Numerous top salespeople are promoted to leadership positions such as general manager or sales manager. However, oftentimes they just don't make the grade. It's frequently assumed that since they were great salespeople, they would naturally be great leaders. But this theory often doesn't hold true.

The word leadership is often used frivolously. After obtaining my degree in leadership, I came to realize that most problems, from organizations to families, are caused by a lack of leadership. Applying effective leadership skills could solve many of these problems.

It's a Lonely Job—*but Somebody Has to Do It*

Sometimes as leaders, we have to go it alone. I discovered recently that, back in the 1960s, one of McDonald's franchisees had developed the Big Mac hamburger recipe. When the head honchos at corporate headquarters found out how this new hamburger was being made, they were totally against it. The bigwigs demanded that the franchisee change the recipe by taking out the middle bun. They also offered a few other changes for the franchisee to incorporate, but to no avail.

He was a maverick. On his own, he went back to using his *original* recipe for the Big Mac, which had been bringing him tremendous success in the first place. He did this without corporate approval. Today, the Big Mac is the most famous hamburger in the world. True leaders must often take big risks.

Leaders *Empower* Their People

When people see the leader, they need to see hope personified. What is hope anyway? It's a feeling that what is wanted will one day happen. The leader's body language needs to radiate hope and say, "We'll get there and I'm going to see to it! We'll all get there together." Body language is a powerful communicator.

As mentioned previously, 93 percent of all human communication is done on a nonverbal level. Our body language speaks volumes about us even before we open our mouth. That's why I encourage leaders everywhere to "walk as if you have some place to go, even when you don't." People will begin to follow you or move out of the way. Don't be surprised when they start holding doors open for you, saying things like, "Oh, let him through. He has some place to go!"

Organizations want leaders who can inspire their people to reach down into their souls and bring out the best that is within themselves. They want leaders who can encourage their people to dream dreams they never believed possible. For true leaders, the word "impossible" is the starting point. It's not used in any other context except to refer to it as: the point at which they need to *start*. That's the motivating power of leadership!

An effective leader takes people to places they've never been before. Leadership is never stagnant. It isn't effective leadership unless it's causing the organization to move forward. Organizations must encourage others to lead the way because leadership is about change. It's about anticipating change, initiating change, and embracing change when it comes. There is no real growth without change, and no real leadership without growth.

The "Facts" *Are Not the Truth*

Many effective leaders encourage their people to ask questions. When we ask questions, we get clarity and elevate our thinking. When we elevate our thinking, we expand our possibilities. When we expand our possibilities, we come to realize that the facts don't count. The facts are only true for us as long as we believe them. We cannot live our lives based solely on facts because facts are changing, *almost daily*. Besides, facts don't motivate us anyway; but possibilities do!

We often hear about how many businesses fail and how "there are no guarantees." These two "facts" don't motivate anyone. On the contrary, if we let them, they deter us from achieving our goals. William Faulkner exclaimed, "Facts and truth really don't have much to do with each other!"

In 1949, when the Federation for the Blind was founded, 99 percent of blind people were unemployed. So, the founders of this organization decided to encourage their members to view blindness as a personality trait rather than a disability. The leaders encouraged their people to rethink what was possible. They *changed* the facts! Because of this paradigm shift, blind people today are succeeding in areas once believed impossible. They are now in almost every field imaginable, including teaching, law, art, Olympic athletics, entertaining, TV talk show hosting, professional speaking, and business ownership. The list goes on and on.

Do you remember Allen Funt from *Candid Camera*? He used to say most people don't ask questions; they just accept things as they are. He said most people just go with the flow without question.

Years ago, the *Candid Camera* crew was in Delaware filming a few segments for the show. They put up a giant sign that read, "Delaware Closed Today." Mr. Funt commented that what was so amazing about the entire episode was that most motorists didn't even question this outrageous sign. Some of them just asked, "Well, uh...is New Jersey open?"

New Times Require *New Thinking*

Robert Kriegel wrote in his book, *If It Ain't Broke. . .Break It!*, "New times call for new thinking. Today, business people have to turn the old rules inside out, upside down and backwards not only to succeed, but to survive." I found that today's economy demands—it almost screams—for new leadership.

Leadership isn't what it used to be. In *Vital Speeches of the Day*, one CEO pointed out, "We can't beat people into the ground anymore." The do-it-because-I'm-in-charge leadership style is antiquated and ineffective. Today, organizations expect more from their leaders. They want leaders who can do at least four key things: 1) *inspire* their people; 2) *encourage* them to believe in the impossible; 3) *be passionate* about their people; and 4) understand that their *actions set the tone* for the entire organization.

Leaders Encourage *Believing in the Impossible*

Since we've already spent a lot of time talking about inspiration, let's briefly look at the other three behaviors that are essential for effective leadership in today's uncertain and unpredictable environment.

Why is *encouraging* team members to believe in the impossible so important for organizational success? Effective leaders know that we can all do more than we *think* we can. "If we all did the things we are capable of doing, we would literally astound ourselves," declared Thomas Edison. Believe it! As human beings, we must constantly be reminded that our capacities can never be measured. Never! Our true potential is limitless. Effective leaders encourage their people to believe in doing the impossible. After all, *we don't know*—we really don't know what ultimately can be achieved. That's the encouraging power of leadership!

The celebrated Romanian gymnastics coach, Bela Karolyi, always encouraged his country's gymnasts to believe in the impossible. Nadia, a little Romanian girl, readily accepted this belief; she didn't want to do what every other gymnast was doing. Her goal was to do what most people said was impossible. As a result of this attitude, she went on to redefine her sport at the 1976 Olympic games in Munich, Germany.

Nadia Comaneci did what most people, at the time, thought was impossible. She scored a perfect 10 on her first gymnastics routine. This was the first time in Olympic competition that a gymnast had ever scored a perfect 10. Keep in mind now, no one thought it was possible to do this! The scoreboards weren't even designed to show 10; they only went up to 9.99.

When Nadia received her first score, the judges were in total agreement that it was a perfect routine. However, they had no way of showing a 10 on a scoreboard that couldn't accommodate two digits before the decimal point. They displayed a score of ten the best way they could, putting up a 1.0 on the board.

The judges took the longest time to come up with this solution. By the time Nadia saw her score she said to herself, "What is this?" She knew she had done much better than to earn only a score of 1.0. Her coach went over to the judges' table to ask for clarification, then he went over to Nadia to share the historic news. At the end of the competition, Nadia Comaneci had received an amazing seven perfect 10s. After the 1976 Olympics, all gymnastics scoreboards had to be redesigned to be able to show a perfect 10.00 score.

My question for you today is this, "Are you ready for the impossible?" As leaders, we must be ready for the impossible. We have to be on the lookout for the impossible. Leaders need to promote the impossible, believe in the impossible, speak the impossible, and expect the impossible.

When Jimmy Carter ran for President of the United States in the mid-1970s, his winning was considered impossible. After telling his mother that he was running for president, her reply was, "President of what, Jimmy?" Even Atlanta's leading newspaper, *The Atlanta Journal-Constitution,* ran a headline that read, "Jimmy is Running for President of What?" Effective leaders know that the old-time saying is true: "It's not what we *know* that gets us into trouble, it's what we *think* we know."

Leaders Are Passionate About Their People

Now, let's talk about why leaders *must* have a *passion*, or love, for their people. Leadership is successful when the people take action! The focus must be on the people. Leadership is a partnership between the leader and the people, which requires the respect and support of those who are being led. The best way for leaders to garner it is by taking care of those who look to them for strength and direction. Leadership, then, is ultimately about winning the hearts of the people.

When I was in the health club business, I worked for a guy named Mark. He was an autocratic kind of leader, more *results* oriented and less *relationship* oriented. He was known for not taking care of his people. For example, I had had a problem with my paycheck being a few hundred dollars short, so Mark's response was, "Well, Spark Plug, we'll just make it up to you on the next pay period." Obviously, this didn't sit too well with me, but he was the boss.

After Mark was transferred to another health club, they brought in a new guy named Kevin. He was more of a laissez-faire type of leader who allowed his people to have more autonomy. Kevin respected us enough to let us do our jobs. He was sharp enough to realize that we already knew what the job entailed. He was always available if we needed assistance, and constantly offered our team encouraging words to help us succeed. Kevin made it a point of taking care of his people.

There was another occasion when my paycheck was a few hundred dollars short; I quickly brought it to Kevin's attention.

Unlike Mark, Kevin replied, "Spark Plug, I'm going over to the corporate office later this afternoon. While I'm there, I'll get another check made out to you for the amount of the short. Is that okay?"

I responded, "Sure. Thanks."

We *worked* for Mark, but we were *loyal* to Kevin. Kevin won our hearts because he loved us.

Leaders who have a passion for their people care about those they are leading.

Leaders' Actions Set the Tone

Organizations want leaders who understand that their actions set the tone for the entire organization. Why is it that General Electric spends upwards of $800 million a year on leadership training and development? They want to set a positive tone for the entire organization. In essence, they are saying that everyone has leadership ability; therefore, they want to provide the necessary environment to nurture it.

Why is leading by example so important for organizational success? People look to their leaders to show them the way. When leaders are trustworthy and listen to the concerns of others, they're setting a tone of integrity and compassion for the entire organization. When leaders are committed to their people, they will follow.

What else can effective leaders do to set the tone for the *entire* organization? They promote what's *good* for the organization by emphasizing the importance of teamwork, quality, hope, creativity, collaboration, enthusiasm, personal and professional development, empowerment, integrity, exceptional customer service, balance between work and family life, embracing people from different cultures, valuing diversity, personal rejuvenation, health, and many other things that can create a more productive and harmonious atmosphere.

Effective leadership needs to be fostered, especially during tough times. Now is the time for you to lead the way. Whether it's on the job, in your home, or in your business, effective leadership makes the difference by improving the lives of the people you are leading and those you otherwise serve.

—12—

Launch Out into the Deep!

"Only one who devotes himself to a cause with his whole strength and soul can be a true master. For this reason, mastery demands all of a person."
—Albert Einstein—

ave you ever thought you would do something great with your life? Do you want to become a leader in your career or business? If so, it will require sacrifice. Prepare to devote sufficient time to whatever you yearn to do.

If you read enough books on any subject or spend enough quality time doing any task, you can become a leader. Repetition is the key. Pledge to stay focused in spite of any interruptions that come your way. If you get sidetracked, get right back in the game.

Focusing on your dream, goal, or objective will make the sacrifice easier to bear. Concentrate on the task at hand even if you would like to be doing something else. It may require meeting ten new people a day or giving five presentations a week. Whatever you decide to do has to be what you eat, live, and breathe. It must be evident in every decision you make and every step you take. Albert Einstein declared, "Only one who devotes himself to a cause with his whole strength and soul can be a true master. For this reason, mastery demands all of a person." Ask yourself, "Am I willing to pay the price? Have I discounted the cost? Am I ready to begin?"

What Are You Waiting For?—*Decide and Take Action!*

Whether your dream is to become a great teacher, a leader in business, or the manager of your department, you must get up and *move* toward your goal. Of all the topics we have discussed, the ideas are ineffective unless we take action. I once heard an actor say at a professional speakers seminar, "Education without application is useless." Action requires responsibility and decision-making. Take action and don't wait around for someone else to get the job done. Growth comes only from taking action. Research has shown that 85 percent of the population is not action-oriented. Scores of people are just sitting on the sidelines, hopelessly waiting for success to come to them. But success doesn't respond to waiting. You must act!

Some people are so overwhelmed when it comes to making a decision that they make no decision at all. Eventually their dream loses its clarity and becomes so dull that they forget how to dream. Believe that your decision to move forward is the right decision. Don't spend your time worrying about taking the wrong action. Either way, you're going to learn something.

Go ahead; decide and take action. Don't let a great opportunity pass you by because of the fear of making a bad decision. Look around and evaluate others who are living life to the fullest. I did this years ago and realized that most people who get things done are not necessarily the best and the brightest. What sets them apart from all the rest is that they simply take action on whatever they want to do. They make up their minds to take action, and stay in the game.

You've got to keep moving! There's no growth to be had in standing still. If you find yourself sitting on the sidelines because of doubt and fear, go forward anyway. That's what leaders do.

Fear—*Something We All Need to Overcome*

Lack of confidence can paralyze us to where we may begin to believe our dream is not worth the effort. We become afraid of what others might think or say. At times, our dream begins to seem unobtainable. We eventually get stuck in the midst of impossibility thinking and lie to ourselves by saying, "Oh, it probably wouldn't have worked out anyway. It just wasn't for me."

In the end, we must take responsibility, abandon the tent of fear and doubt, and get moving again. Pledge that you are going to take the first step no matter what. Remember, perfection is a mirage that will prevent you from moving at all. Just get started! Henri Frederic Amiel said, "The man who insists upon seeing with perfect clearness before he decides, never decides." Start now. Work out the details later.

Move now. Get up now. Commit now. Take action—*now!* See obstacles as opportunities turned inside out. Martin Luther proclaimed, "Even if I knew that tomorrow the world would go to pieces, I would still plant my apple tree." As you take that first step, as I'm sure you will, it doesn't matter whether or not you see any immediate results. Do something that will move you toward your destination. The most important thing for you to concentrate on is moving toward your goal. You've stopped hanging around the edge of life's ocean of possibilities and have decided to launch out into the deep. Most often, that which you are seeking is also seeking you. Be on time for your appointment. Don't let another moment slip away.

Time Waits for No One

Carl Sandburg said, "Time is the coin of your life. It is the only coin you have, and only you can determine how it will be spent. Be careful lest you let other people spend it for you." Our time is precious and irreplaceable. The clock never stops ticking. Look at your life as though you're on an incredibly important mission—because you are. So, use your time wisely. A billion dollars cannot replace even one wasted second!

"At first, I was dying to finish high school so I could start college. Then I was dying to finish college so I could start working. Then I was dying to get married so I could have a child. Then I was dying for my child to grow old enough so I could return to work. Then I was dying to retire. Now, I am dying and suddenly, I realized... I forgot to live."

—Unknown

—13—

Remember to Live!

*"The tragedy of life is not death, but what dies
inside while we are living."*
—Norman Cousins—

In our hurry-up world, it's unfortunate that the things that were once considered important for many of us are no longer top priority. But necessities such as fruitful relationships, taking time to know our neighbors, staying in contact with loved ones, and spending time with our families are still important. But now they require appointments. Dr. Rachel Naomi Remen has pointed out that "Most of us live homeless in the neighborhood of our true selves." The majority of us claim that our families are most important. But when we take a closer look at the things we say we believe, many times they don't match up with how we live our lives.

I end my presentations by encouraging the audience to take some time out of their busy lives to have fun with their families and loved ones. Find a place to relax and unwind, even if it's in your local area. Escape to where you can refocus, reenergize yourself, and get back in touch with the ones you love and your dreams. Whether it's at a park, a tennis court, the mountains, the beach, the gym, or the theatre, get out and do something to reconnect with what's truly important to you. Make sure it's special, not just part of your regular routine.

A while back, I heard some shocking news: The average person experiences only about fourteen different things in their entire lives. I said to myself, "How can this be?" As I began thinking about it, I concluded that many people have carved out an everyday routine for their lives. They drive to work the same way every day; watch TV; get something to eat; check their mail, e-mail, and voicemail; go to bed and wake up the next morning to do it all over again. It's no wonder why so many people go in to work with the attitude: "Another boring day"—year in, year out.

After speaking to a group at Hartsfield International Airport, a gentleman informed me that he had been driving to work the same way for the past twenty years. He promised me that he was going to start taking a different route to and from work every once in a while. He said after all those years, he never really gave it any thought.

Are You Sitting Down with the Remote?

Don't be sitting down with the remote control, letting life pass you by. Throw the remote away. Stop watching *other* people become successful. Get up and take charge of your future!

Add more passion and excitement to your life. Ask yourself, "What do I really love to do, and how am I going to create the lifestyle so I can to do it?" Do you remember the song called *Sailing* by Christopher Cross? The lyrics are so calming. "Sailing takes me away to where I've always heard it could be, just a dream and the wind to carry me, soon I will be free." Christopher must love sailing or what it symbolizes to write such a beautiful song about it. What do you love to do so much that you could write a song about it? What is it for you? What activity do you enjoy so much that when you're doing it, all else seems right with the world?

After speaking for a group in Boston, a gentleman came up to me and shared this interesting tidbit: "Mr. Spark Plug, it doesn't matter how tough my day has been at work, when I go home, I can pick up my saxophone, start playing, and all else seems right with the world."

My wife and I have a special paradise-like place about sixty miles south of Atlanta where we go to relax and get away from the hustle and bustle of life. A peaceful, serene oasis for the entire family, it's called Callaway Gardens. Fourteen thousand magnificent acres of flowers, walking paths, bicycle trails, a butterfly conservatory, golf, picnic areas, restaurants, villas, chalets, tennis courts, vegetable gardens, lakes, streams, a man-made beach, and many other amenities help us relax and unwind. There is seldom a traffic jam.

Where would you love to go? How long will it be before you get there? What are you waiting for? Do whatever it takes to create a lifestyle in which you can afford to do so.

We especially love going to the beach. So much so, that Jacqueline even has a collection of shells from the world's most beautiful beaches. We also love the mountains and state parks.

Norman Cousins wrote, "The tragedy of life is not death, but what dies inside while we are living." Has the desire to live your life with passion died inside of you? If it has, it's never too late to wake up and live! It has been documented that many people who have been diagnosed with cancer, credit their diagnosis for inspiring them to actually live abundant lives. What a paradox! It sometimes takes a would-be death sentence to inspire us to live.

Research has also shown that those who follow their creative passions actually live longer. The first time I heard this, I thought about the late Frank Lloyd Wright, one of the twentieth century's best-known and most respected architects. His busiest time in his professional life was his early nineties. He said, "The longer I live, the more beautiful life becomes." He had a passion for his work that had never been seen in an architect before.

When my wife and I were visiting the Grand Canyon a few years ago, we marveled at its grandeur, majesty, and beauty. While in Arizona, we saw the beautiful red rocks of Sedona and the Painted Desert, and also visited Taliesin West, Frank Lloyd Wright's desert masterpiece and his home. Mr. Wright believed that his creations needed to become a part of nature, not compete with it. We could definitely see and feel the passion he had for his craft while visiting his magnificent home.

Grandma Moses, the famous painter, didn't begin her painting career until she was in her early seventies. Some of the world's greatest artists did their best work near the end of their lives. This includes people such as Monet, Renoir, Matisse, and many others. If we want more out of life, we must find something to be passionate about. It's never too late to start living life with passion!

If my grandmother can still be living her life with passion, I have no excuse. At eighty-nine, she's as busy as ever. She's a twenty-five year member of the Live Long & Like It Club. I guess their motto is: If you're going to live long, you may as well like it! My wife and I can hardly keep up with her. She's always on the go.

I remember calling her once saying, "Granny, we want to come down to Jacksonville to see you next weekend."

She replied, "Oh no, Sugah, y'all can't come and see me next weekend 'cause we're all taking a cruise to the Bahamas."

I replied, "Bahamas?"

Granny responded, "Oh, yeah, we're going to the Bahamas." And then I inquired about the following weekend.

"I can't see y'all the following weekend, either Sugah, 'cause we're all going to Ft. Lauderdale for dinner." She asked, "You still have the key, don't you, Sugah?"

"Yes, ma'am," I said.

She replied, "Y'all come on down and make yourselves at home, I just won't be here. I know you young folks can find *something* to do."

The lesson I learned from Granny is that you're never too old to live a passionate, exciting life. Isn't it time you added more passion and excitement to yours?

I'd like to share some age-old advice from a new friend I made a couple years ago. Her name is Dr. Leila Denmark and she's 108 years old! She was born on February 1, 1898. Dr. Denmark closed her medical practice in January 2002 at the remarkable age of 103, after more than seventy years of happily serving the metro-Atlanta community. She is a well-respected, legendary pediatrician.

Dr. Denmark was the first intern at Egleston Children's Hospital in Atlanta, and the third female graduate from the Medical College of Georgia in 1928. She was named Atlanta's Woman of the Year for 1953.

As we sat in her spacious library on our very first visit to her home, Dr. Denmark gave us an oral history about her life and shared some nuggets of wisdom on how *we* can create a better life. Her husband was the vice president of the Federal Reserve Bank in Atlanta, and with all her professional and financial success, she shared the following words: "Always remember, money doesn't mean a thing unless you're happy."

As you can see, at 108, Dr. Denmark has lived a truly fruitful life. I asked her if she could do it all over again, what would she do differently. Without hesitation, her reply was, "Spark Plug, I wouldn't change a thing under the sun; I've lived a good long life!" And what a life it has been. Thanks for the inspiration, Dr. Denmark.

"When you're dying, when you turn that sharp corner and suddenly realize not only there is an end but that this is also the end, all your obsessions with security and status and time spent doing anything other than what you really want to do, or must do, often seem ludicrous."

—Gregg Levoy

—14—

You've Got What It Takes!

"We cannot become what we need to be by remaining what we are."
—Max DuPree—

You have what it takes to make it through any situation. Think prosperity, not lack of money; freedom, not bondage; love, not hate; peace, not turmoil. Focus on what *can be* for you, your family, and your organization. Refuse to sit idly by and just accept what life hands you. Kathleen Andrus said, "The bottom line is that I am responsible for my own well-being, my own happiness. The choices and decisions I make regarding my life directly influence the quality of my days."

I know there is always more to achieve, more to experience, and more to give. To think any other way is to work against the plan and mission for our lives. Though you may not yet be living the life that's possible for you, that doesn't mean you can't make it happen. Keep the fire burning. Keep creating a larger vision for your life by pushing beyond your doubts and fears. As Frank Scully asked, "Why not go out on a limb; isn't that where the fruit is?"

Take advantage of the opportunity that's now in your hands. Wouldn't it be sad if you reached the end of your years without moving beyond where you are right now? Wouldn't it be sad if you didn't stretch your abilities as far as they could take you? Wouldn't it be a shame if you didn't become all you were meant to be?

Author Gregg Levoy summed it up best saying, "When you're dying, when you turn that sharp corner and suddenly realize not only there is *an* end but that this is also *the* end, all your obsessions with security and status and time spent doing anything other than what you really want to do, or must do, often seem ludicrous."

There are no limitations for us except those we place on ourselves. If you have the desire, that's reason enough to know you can accomplish whatever you set out to do.

Carl Weathers, best known as Apollo Creed in the *Rocky* movie series, was asked in an interview, "What would you do if you weren't an actor?"

Without hesitation he replied, "I would be trying to get into acting." His love of acting was that strong.

You are your own artist; you have the power to paint your own picture. No one can paint it as colorfully and creatively as you can. No one else will place the same strokes on the canvas that you can. Your destiny has only *your* name on it! As the Olympian twins, Calvin and Alvin Harrison said, "We must make up our mind to go to *our* destiny. If we don't *go*, our destiny will never be fulfilled."

There are times in our lives when we must take that giant leap of faith into unfamiliar territory. We've got to sometimes walk where there are no trails and journey into the unknown. Be willing to take chances. Max DuPree proclaimed, "We cannot become what we need to be by remaining what we are."

People often give up and drop out of the game too soon. Harriet Beecher Stowe wrote these encouraging words: "When you get into a tight place and everything goes against you, till it seems as though you could not hold on a minute longer, never give up then, for that is just the place and time that the tide will turn." Remember Shirley Caesar's song, *You're Next in Line for a Miracle!* You may be close to crossing the finish line, but you'll never know it if you throw in the towel. If you quit, you'll live the miserable and unfulfilled life of *what could have been.*

Sure the load gets heavy, times get a little tough, the way gets a little bleak and, at times, it may be difficult to find support for your endeavors. You're definitely going to get tired sometimes, and every once in a while it will seem as if everything has come to a screeching halt. Keep the faith! Many of life's challenging experiences are just some of the perks of being a card-carrying member of the human race. Whatever you are experiencing in life, someone has already endured it and gone on to overcome many seemingly insurmountable obstacles. You don't have to be superhuman to face life head-on. You can handle it!

When It's All Said and Done

After all is said and done, we will be remembered for our attitude toward others. A few years ago, while my wife and I were visiting a nursing home, I had the pleasure of meeting a wonderful ninety-two-year-old lady. I stopped by her room just to say hello. She graciously invited me in and offered me a chair. I took a seat in front of her and could tell by the look on her face that she was excited about having a new visitor. We began our conversation.

We talked about everything—where she was born, where she lived, where she traveled, and what she liked and disliked; this went on for about a half-hour or so. She then told me that she had been married for fifty-three years before her husband had passed away. She was so devastated that she could no longer live alone. That's what brought her to the nursing home.

I was impressed with the number of years she had been married. At that time, I had been married for only about five years.

I then inquired, "Ma'am, after fifty-three years of marriage, what do you remember the most about your husband?" As she contemplated my question, I noticed a faint smile beginning to show on her small face, and there was a little twinkle in her eye.

She took a deep breath and responded in a soft and sincere voice, "What I remember the most about my husband was his goodness and kindness."

I was touched by her response. After fifty-three years of marriage, she didn't say she remembered the kind of clothes he wore, the car he drove, the home they lived in, or the amount of money they had. All she remembered, as a ninety-two-year-old lady in that nursing home, was his goodness and kindness. What do you want people to remember about you?

We trust that you will continue your journey of self-discovery. Go ahead...get ready to face the day with renewed confidence. Hold your head up high, pull your shoulders back. Your dream is priceless and within your reach. You will find that unlimited possibilities await those who have discovered the awesome power of digging down a little deeper when times are tough. Your dream is worth the struggle. Pursuing it will cause you to—*grow through it and lead!*

"*It's so easy to lose sight of your goals and ambitions.*

The interruptions and struggles seem to interfere with your mission.

And sometimes you may even come to the conclusion that your dream in reality is just an illusion.

But twists and turns are only parts of the plan.

Even when you fall, you can rise again.

My advice to you is hold on for awhile.

A breakthrough can be in the very next mile.

And then one day, it will be clear to see that to simply hold on is the ultimate key."

—Jacqueline Benjamin Thomas

Who Are Anthony "The Spark Plug" Thomas and Jacqueline Benjamin Thomas?

Anthony "The Spark Plug" Thomas, is the president of Spark Plug International, a professional keynote speaking and consulting company. When ACDelco, America's leading manufacturer of spark plugs, needed a "human spark plug" to inspire their salespeople, they called "The *(original)* Spark Plug."

"The Spark Plug" has been wowing audiences since 1995 with insightful, inspirational, informative, and entertaining messages on life, growing, leadership, diversity, and motivation. His dynamic messages have been heard here and abroad by organizations such as General Motors, AT&T, Sheraton Hotels, ADP, U.S. Postal Service, BellSouth, Georgia Power, ACDelco, Southern Company, Lucent Technologies, and others. He has traveled to twenty countries, and is also a U.S. Navy veteran, art collector, tennis player, mentor, snow skier, biking enthusiast, and real estate investor. He has a voice that touches the soul.

A distinguished graduate of Mercer University with a degree in organization leadership and Duke University's leadership program, "The Spark Plug" uses real-life lessons and unchangeable, time-tested principles to inspire people to dip deeply into the well of their souls, draw out their gifts and talents, and then put them to use. When asked why he wrote this book, "The Spark Plug" says, "'The late Leo Rosten wrote, 'The purpose of life is to matter, to be productive, to be useful, to have it make some difference that you lived at all.' I hope this book inspires readers to make a difference." He lives with his wife, Jacqueline, and their niece in Georgia. Visit him at www.sparkplug1.com.

Jacqueline, the creative force behind the success of Spark Plug International, has a degree in management and computer science. She is also an artist, freelance writer, graphic designer, author, publisher, poet, consultant, and presentation coach.

When she isn't hammering away at her computer, you just might find her enjoying her passion for reading, hiking in the mountains, or meditating on new ideas.